CW01662356

Cyber for ***Builders***

The Essential Guide to Building a Cybersecurity Startup

Ross Haleliuk

ISBN: 978-1-7382341-0-3

Imprint: Venture in Security Press

Publisher: Venture in Security Press

Cover Design: Miscreants (www.miscreants.com)

Formatting and Layout: Scott McFarlane

Contents

Cyber for ***Builders***

Foreword

by Caleb Sima

In "Cyber for Builders," Ross Haleliuk offers a concise and essential guide for aspiring builders in the cybersecurity industry. Drawing from his extensive experience as a product leader, Ross provides invaluable insights into the business side of cybersecurity.

This book stands out by focusing on the intersection of technology, business, and market dynamics within the cybersecurity ecosystem. It covers critical topics, such as understanding investors, building winning teams, and designing effective go-to-market strategies. What sets it apart is its emphasis on thinking outside the box and challenging conventional playbooks. Ross highlights the need for adaptability and creative problem-solving to build the companies that the world needs today.

Whether you're an aspiring founder, security engineer, product manager, or investor, this book is an essential resource to navigate the complex landscape of cybersecurity. Ross's practical advice and real-world examples empower readers to make informed decisions and drive meaningful change in this ever-evolving field.

As a founder, investor, and CSO with over 25 years of experience in the cybersecurity industry, "Cyber for Builders" by Ross Haleliuk has captivated me with its remarkable and insightful content. Ross's unique perspective, shaped by his deep understanding of the field, shines through every chapter.

His valuable insights continue to surprise even seasoned professionals like myself, making it not just a book, but a roadmap for those passionate about building a safer and more secure digital future.

> Caleb Sima is a renowned cybersecurity expert and a pioneer in application security. He has founded successful cybersecurity companies, served in key security leadership roles, and made significant contributions to the industry. Sima's expertise is evidenced by his patents, influential book, and leadership in the cybersecurity community. He continues to shape the industry through his innovative approach as he chairs the CSA AI Security Initiative. His career embodies a visionary blend of technical mastery and strategic insight..

Foreword

by Jeremiah Grossman

Bruce Schneier once said, "Security is both a feeling and a reality, and they're different. You can feel secure even though you're not, and you can be secure even though you don't feel it." As an entrepreneur, it's important to apply this concept to security controls (i.e. firewalls, vulnerability management, antivirus, etc). Some security controls provide substantial protection, but may not evoke a tangible feeling of security. Other controls make people feel secure, but don't necessarily enhance actual security (these are generally mocked and referred to as "security theater"). A simple example to understand the distinction is encryption. Encryption increases security, but it's the little "green lock" icon in the web browser that helps people feel like they're being protected. As trivial as this may appear, appreciating the distinction is paramount in making informed decisions about information security strategy, investments, and business success. How well a security control improves a person's feeling of security can actually be more important than creating an effective product. The simple fact is, no one will listen to or buy anything from someone unless they first provide peace of mind — no matter how truly effective their product is. As a thought exercise, think beyond information security on the security-related things in life that you buy, and don't buy, based on a feeling of security. What do you notice?

The challenge we have in the current culture of cybersecurity is that most practitioners are conditioned to focus on and only respect security controls intended to reduce risk. And for some reason, there's scarce time or respect given to the 'feelings' of the people we're responsible for protecting. Our space has a reputation for condescension and frustration with the general masses who just don't automatically listen and comply. For information security practitioners and entrepreneurs alike, this blind spot is a huge gap that limits the impact and success they could otherwise have. Similar to "security WITH obscurity," we should "feel secure AND be secure."

I have personally seen a number of potentially great companies with great teams and great products fail simply because they didn't provide peace of mind. And, while still being brilliant engineers, they didn't fully appreciate the value of telling their story in a compelling way to people who know far less than they do. As Steve Jobs once said, "The most powerful person in the world is the storyteller. The storyteller sets the vision, values and agenda of an entire generation that is to come." Do not ignore this lesson.

Over the last couple of decades, many cybersecurity vendors have spent vast sums of money on marketing campaigns and conference parties as their go-to-market strategy. Some have successfully executed this way. Their campaigns are generally designed to do 3 things: 1) Get attention. 2) Create urgency. 3) Provide peace of mind. That's it. And they do so while accepting that they're hocking products that simply don't work or don't deliver as promised. We call them "snake oil", and our industry is filled with such examples.

Any security practitioner with any amount of integrity will find this business strategy offensive. This is effectively a scam, and when it comes to InfoSec, it also risks hurting a lot of people in the process. Setting this aside, the crucial lesson remains that in the real world, people in their hearts still value peace of mind above and beyond the promise of security and risk reduction. Judge people harshly if you like, but the fact remains and it's something to be mindful of. Fortunately, there is no good reason to choose between the feeling of security and actual security. Offer both! That's what the best security controls and the most successful InfoSec companies provide.

Ross's book already provides a great framework for building a great company with a great product, so I'm going to focus on ways to provide people with peace of mind. Before diving in, there are a few more lessons about InfoSec we must discuss further.

- InfoSec is designed, built, and maintained by people. People who have lives, money, and secrets to protect. People who have jobs and reputations to protect. People who want people to look out for them, and have their back when/if disaster strikes. At the end of the day, InfoSec is people.

- InfoSec is highly complex, scary, and constantly evolving. No one can claim a high level of expertise in anything but the smallest fraction of the overall knowledge base. We instinctively know this is the case and act accordingly by relying upon the expertise of those who have distinguished in a particular niche and earned our trust.
- InfoSec is a marketplace of niche expertise and point solutions. When technology advances (i.e. the cloud, SaaS, AI/ML) there's always another attack surface people will have to build products to protect. And then, when our security controls work, the adversaries (again, they're people, too) will shift their strategy or tactics.

With these aspects in mind, my process to provide peace of mind (and build a great product) begins by focusing on clearly defining a particular problem, a problem that was personally important to me. Then, I would intensely study absolutely everything there was to study on the topic. I'd collaborate regularly with every expert in the space and ask them every question I could think of. Taking careful note of any time they said, "I don't know," as that was the edge of knowledge. Then I'd teach others what I learned or figured out by publishing content and public speaking all the time, everywhere — obsessively.

At one point in my career, I was focused on application security. The problem I identified was that there were millions upon millions of websites littered with vulnerabilities that needed to be found and fixed before they were exploited, but no one knew how to do this at scale. The scale of the problem is what made solving it both interesting, and a lucrative business opportunity. When I founded WhiteHat Security, I studied, wrote, and reviewed code, hacked everything, spoke publicly, authored books, blogged, engaged on social media, and evangelized nonstop about nothing but application security for years and years. More than anyone else. This effort earned me a reputation for being a leading expert in the field and people increasingly listened to what I had to say and what I recommended. Combined with building the best application security product on the market, peace of mind resulted as a natural byproduct. I've used the exact same playbook with topics such as cyber insurance, EDR and ransomware, attack surface management, and so on.

Of course, the personal expertise and reputations of the company founders aren't the only way for a company to establish credibility with buyers and provide them with peace of mind. Some startups will offer customers free or deeply discounted products and services in exchange for testimonials or references. Some will leverage the reputations of high-profile people by adding them to their company boards. Others will apply for industry awards and five-star product reviews. They'll pay for coverage or a report from industry analysts. Pick the methods that suit you best as it all comes down to building credibility, which provides peace of mind.

The bottom line is there's a delicate balance between feeling secure and being secure in the realm of information security and entrepreneurship. Entrepreneurs must navigate this complex landscape by investing in measures that not only provide genuine protection but also foster a perceptible sense of security. This nuanced approach is imperative for establishing trust with customers. The dialogue between perception and reality in information security is not only a technical challenge, but a strategic imperative that separates successful businesses and bankruptcy.

Jeremiah Grossman is an investor and security leader, previously Co-Founder and CEO of Bit Discovery, and Founder of WhiteHat Security. Jeremiah's career spans over 20 years and he has lived a literal lifetime in computer security to become one of the industry's biggest names. In 2001, Jeremiah founded WhiteHat Security, which today has one of the largest professional hacking armies on the planet. Jeremiah has received a number of industry awards, been publicly thanked by Microsoft, Mozilla, Google, Facebook, and many others for privately informing them of weaknesses in their systems - a polite way of saying, "hacking them". Jeremiah has been featured in the Wall Street Journal, Forbes, NY Times and hundreds of other media outlets around the world who rely upon his expertise.

Preface

If you were to ask me a decade ago where I see myself working in the future, the answer would have been anything but cybersecurity. As someone who has always enjoyed building - businesses, products, communities, and relationships, I choose to specialize in product management for several reasons. First, I knew that when the time was right, I would build my own startup, and working in product management appeared to provide the most well-rounded perspective for a future founder. Second, I found it to be quite broad as a discipline and therefore a great fit for a generalist like myself. Product management encompasses all elements of the product lifecycle from customer discovery, customer support, customer relationship management, engineering, legal, sales, partnership, and operations, to finance, team building, analytics, and design, to name a few. Third, it allowed me to grow while moving from one industry to another until I found the field I would like to stay in for the long term. Lastly, compared to other functional areas of business, it paid quite well and had great prospects for both personal and professional growth.

Having worked in retail, wholesale, e-commerce, and fintech, I was fortunate to develop a broad view of the tech industry, the ability to zoom in and zoom out, and to see patterns where others saw seemingly unrelated events. These skills and perspectives became invaluable when in 2021, I joined LimaCharlie as a Head of Product to focus on go-to-market strategy and building an innovative security platform customers love.

My approach has always been the same: to pick a problem worth solving, and go all-in. During my fintech days, three months after joining a startup that was reinventing the homebuyers' journey, I became a licensed mortgage broker. During the first few months at LimaCharlie, I was absorbing everything I could about the cybersecurity space by talking to as many people as possible, attending events, listening to podcasts, reading articles and books, and having deep conversations with any cyber-focused investor, practitioner, or security leader who was open to a good chat.

Very quickly, I realized that while there were a lot of great materials about the technical side of security (security engineering, detection engineering, vulnerability management, etc.), the business of security was barely being discussed. Recognizing the need, I started Venture in Security - a blog about the business side of cybersecurity, trends defining the direction of the industry, and how different components and actors fit together. The goal was to help cybersecurity practitioners, founders, and investors shape the future of the industry. Almost every week, I would share thoughts and learnings covering everything from go-to-market strategies, open source, security services, channel partners, venture capital, angel investing, product-led growth, and much more. The response was phenomenal. When the first 500 people signed up to receive a weekly newsletter, I thought to myself "That's unexpected". Then, there were 1,000, then 2,000, then 5,000, then 10,000, and then I just stopped counting. As the readership grew, so did my realization that understanding the business side of security is critical to innovate. We cannot push the industry to advance and mature unless passionate software and security engineers continue to expand the boundaries of what's possible and look for better ways to protect the digital world from malicious actors seeking to wreak havoc and cause destruction.

For a long time, I've been asked by many of the Venture in Security readers if I am planning to publish a book; every time I would dismiss the question, saying something like "Yeah, someday". I started condensing hundreds of individual posts and articles and putting together a mini-book that any busy founder or aspiring entrepreneur could refer to as they embark on a journey of building a company. You are now holding this book in your hands. Written to be as concise as possible, it summarizes my learnings over the years and attempts to provide a foundational understanding of how the security industry works, who the different players are, and how their interactions shape what we know as a business of security, what to keep in mind when designing the go-to-market strategy, how to think about building the team and raising capital, how to scale, and what trends shape the industry.

Most cybersecurity books are written for hackers, security leaders and practitioners, and a general audience. This book is different as it is intended first and foremost for builders - founders, security engineers, marketing and sales teams, product managers, VCs, angel investors, software developers, investor relations and analyst relations professionals, and others who are building the future of cybersecurity. While almost anyone interested in a better understanding of the mechanics that shape the security space can learn something new by reading this book, I hope that it will be especially useful to security practitioners tinkering with new ideas and considering building a security company.

This book was primarily written for product builders. Although there will be cases when I am going to be mentioning service companies, and I do believe that we need many more service providers as they are in many ways the future of security, I was mostly thinking about building product startups (it is something I am familiar with and passionate about). Moreover, I am mostly focusing on B2B enterprise companies for the US market. I will discuss other market segments where appropriate and fully recognize that the world is bigger than the US, and in different countries, the buying habits, industry participants, suppliers of capital, and other parties might look different (or be completely absent), however, the US is what I am most prepared to discuss. In my blog, I sometimes write about other markets such as Europe - you can check Venture in Security (www.ventureinsecurity.net) for more.

The book is split into six sections:

- Section one covers the foundations of cybersecurity as an industry.
- Section two provides an overview of the several important players that shape current-day cybersecurity - investors (angel investors, angel networks, angel syndicates, VCs, and corporate VCs), influencers (analyst firms, regulators, and insurance companies), distributors (channel partners), and acquirers (product and service companies from within and outside of the industry).

- Section three discusses several trends defining the future of cybersecurity.
- Section four offers a selection of mental models and notes to help early-stage cybersecurity founders get their ideas off the ground.
- Section five provides a look into factors that often kill cybersecurity startups.
- Section six calls for founders to break playbooks when building their companies.

As you navigate through the book, you will notice that it includes contributions by 50+ cybersecurity entrepreneurs, operators, thought leaders, and investors. Where appropriate, I added QR codes that link to relevant articles in my blog for readers interested in learning more about the topic.

It's time to build.

SECTION 1

Security as an industry: essential overview

To discuss different players and the dynamics in the cybersecurity space, it is important to first establish a shared understanding of what security as an industry is. This section will provide this understanding, and answer adjacent questions such as what makes security unique compared to other fields, and what other important characteristics of the space are.

Cybersecurity is a horizontal, not a vertical

Market analysts like to compare cybersecurity to other fields such as fintech, agritech, and martech. Although the desire to categorize, label everything, and assign a clearly defined bucket is understandable, in the case of security it doesn't serve us well. This is because cybersecurity is a horizontal, not a vertical. Defending the confidentiality, integrity, and availability of data is a cross-industry, cross-technological, and cross-customer need. Whether we are talking about space exploration or mining, education or healthcare, AI or ML, 3D printing or virtual reality, multinational corporations or charities, every one of them needs to be secured.

Some people think about it and say "Well, don't other fields also help our society run more efficiently? How about, say, payments infrastructure?". Although there are indeed other core knowledge areas and industries, what makes cybersecurity unique is the fact that it is not a separate functionality which everything needs to interact with. Instead, it is a fundamental part of what everything is. While one payment provider can be replaced with another, and in some cases, the product can be offered for free, thus making payment processing unnecessary, the same cannot be done for security. Security is a part of the way software is architected and built, a part of the way relationships between different entities are conceived, and the way different parties interact with one another, and as such, it cannot be seen as a stand-alone technology that can be "replaced" or separated from the core value offering. Security needs to be designed and built in.

Cybersecurity has an external force of innovation

Another factor that makes security unique is that the pace of innovation in this field is tied to three aspects:

1. Tech innovation at large.
2. Competitive landscape.
3. Threat actor activity.

Most industries only need to deal with the first two of the three factors. For example, when the cloud gained widespread adoption, it pushed companies across different verticals to adapt to the new technology. Moreover, it gave rise to the new generation of cloud-native players displacing their counterparts who had built their tooling for the on-prem world. The competitive landscape factor is also fairly self-explanatory: as one startup comes up with an innovative way to solve a problem, it pushes those competing with it to catch up.

The third aspect, threat actor activity, is unique: aside from cybersecurity, it can only be seen in conventional warfare where it takes the form of an arms race. This external force means that someone smart on the other side of the wire is actively trying to break into something a company is building or trying to defend. The actors on the offense have the initiative, are well-funded, and are often better motivated. Unlike security teams which get paid annual salaries, attackers will only make money when they accomplish their goals. Then, there's another big set of players, namely nation states, that are often looking to achieve intellectual property, warfare and diplomatic advantages, destabilize a competitor nation, or attain some national security objective.

The product cycles in security are relatively short, and to get closer to innovation, it is important to be closer to the offense. What is talked about in offensive circles today, will be discussed at defensive conferences tomorrow. This is one of the reasons why it is hard to build companies or invest in this space without a strong background in security or a willingness to become a part of the security community. A cybersecurity founder or investor needs to be a part of the security ecosystem, attend events, and stay on top of recent developments, be it business or technology, while also paying attention to what the threat actors are doing.

Expert Insight

"Major technological disruptions are another driver of the security ecosystem. Just when we knew how to manage security in our data centers for client-server architectures, we shifted to the cloud which disrupted everything. It is a universal truth that new tech is deployed without serious thought to security. We have seen many of these trends, from the Internet, to smartphones, to the cloud, to the Internet of Things, and most dramatically, the rise of large language models. There are hundreds of 'cloud security' companies and 161 IoT security specialist companies. To quote John Pescatore: 'Security is never the next Big Thing. But, it is always part of the next Big Thing.'"

- Richard Stiennon, Chief Research Analyst at IT-Harvest

Deep Dive

To learn more about the business side of cybercrime, check out a Venture in Security deep dive titled "The Upside Down: making sense of the business models, organizational structure, and the economy of the cybercrime". You can find it by navigating to https://ventureinsecurity.net/p/the-upside-down-making-sense-of-the or by scanning this QR code.

The quality of what is bought and sold is not known

Another factor that makes cybersecurity particularly unusual is that the quality of what is being bought and sold is unknown. When a finance team is choosing a point of sale (POS), there is a well-understood and testable set of functionality a good product should have; the same is true with most enterprise solutions. On the other hand, a team buying a security product is paying for a promise that a vendor will "keep them safe" and has no way of being certain that in critical moments, the product will do what it promises to do. The overall return on investment (ROI) for security solutions is also always in question. Even in those rare cases when the tool's functionality can be thoroughly tested at the time of purchase, the security team has no way to test the product against attacks that are not yet known.

Because of this inability to be certain that the product will work when it needs to work, buyers look at other factors to see if they can trust the vendor, including:

- The responsiveness of the team, the speed with which they add new capabilities, fix bugs, and answer customers' questions.
- The integrity of the founders, their willingness to build relationships and think long-term instead of maximizing short-term outcomes.
- The signs that the company will be around a year or two later. This is often judged by looking at the founders' background,

their ability to attract strong employees, as well as the presence and reputation of investors.

The fact that the quality of what is bought and sold is unknown, makes switching vendors hard. Most security teams cannot evaluate all possible tools in-house, hence why analyst firms hold a lot of power in the industry and greatly influence purchasing decisions (I will be discussing this topic later).

Heavy reliance on trust has many far-reaching consequences

Everything in cybersecurity relies on trust. The significance of trust becomes evident during the very first day of the company's existence: it takes time for a new startup to establish a trusted relationship with early adopters who can become its first customers or design partners. The reason trust is so critical is the level of impact cybersecurity solutions have on the enterprise: if a startup's product fails to prevent what it was designed to prevent, the consequences for the customer can be catastrophic. Moreover, the security company itself can become a Trojan Horse if it gets exploited by malicious actors (a case in point is the story of Codecov). These are just some of the reasons why relatively few security leaders are comfortable being guinea pigs for new solutions, and why everyone is looking for reference customers, SOC2 compliance, and a long list of signs that someone credible already trusts the product.

The problem of trust also manifests itself in longer sales cycles, comprehensive trials, small-scale initial deployments, and other unique characteristics of the buying process in security. All of this combined leads to a chain reaction with far-reaching consequences. It takes a long time for innovations in the industry to become mainstream. Blitzscaling (moving fast to capture the market) isn't a thing for cybersecurity innovations: in B2B, companies take time to develop confidence in new solutions, while in B2C few individuals are willing to spend money on security at all. This, in turn, means that by the time a new approach to security is mainstream, tens (or even hundreds) of entrepreneurs around the world have learned about the original idea, and built a "me too" company backed by investors looking for a chance to place a bet in a "hot" space. Since the startup that initially pioneered the new approach or the solution had to educate the market about the problem, it 1) was at a disadvantage, 2) had to pick a narrow and well-targeted customer segment to start with, knowing that its resources are limited, and 3) could not establish a trusted relationship with a large number of prospects. All this has likely enabled many "me too" companies to spring across different geographies, market sub-segments, and industry verticals. Not everyone can come up with a new idea, but most can think of a way to build an already existing idea for a somewhat different customer.

Trust is also an important factor when it comes to buying security tools from other countries. While ideas and innovation can and do happen anywhere around the globe, an American company will always prefer a US-based security provider, a French company will buy from French startups, etc. While cybersecurity innovation is global, trust isn't.

This slow and trust-based cycle of new product adoption in cybersecurity means that no single company can capture a large percentage of the market. In many industries, one or a few businesses that move fast, end up dominating the space (think cloud or personal computers). In cybersecurity, no single leader has a double-digit market share: the largest cybersecurity players today own less than 10% of the total market (there are, however, leaders that own a large percentage of different market segments).

Companies in security don't fail at the same rate as in other industries

The trust-based product adoption and slow sales cycles mean that instead of having a few companies that take the market by storm, we typically see several cybersecurity startups solving the same problem operating in parallel and generating enough revenue to survive. This explains another observation: cybersecurity ventures do not fail at the same rate as startups in other industries. While some that don't reach traction do inevitably end up folding, most will find at least a handful of loyal customers, just enough to stick around for years, and sometimes decades. A few will grow fast, but many will end up making enough money for their founders to live comfortable lives and not have to go back to a job (unless their VCs will push them to grow or die quickly).

Although the conventional wisdom driven by the investor expectations of growth may consider these a failure, it comes down to the goals founders established for their entrepreneurial ventures. If all they want is the ability to build cool tech and get paid roughly the same they'd get on the market but without having to deal with management, human resources, and performance reviews, they may very well see this "lifestyle business" as a success.

From the outside, failure to build a large cybersecurity company can often look like success. This is because of the frequency of acquisitions and the fact that many startups that built a usable product, or a rockstar team, can still get bought (commonly for an undisclosed amount). Larger, more mature, or better-funded players are constantly looking to add new capabilities to their portfolios. These facts and the resulting M&A activity in the security market enable founders to sell their struggling venture and start a new one relatively quickly - armed with all the learnings, connections, and a much stronger profile of the "second-time founder" who successfully exited their first company.

Continuous influx of capital prevents natural selection

During the pandemic, cybersecurity was one of the fastest-growing fields. First, companies realized that their existing infrastructure and security practices were not designed with remote work in mind. Second, as people were moving to work from home, cybercriminals seized the opportunity, leading to a rise in the number of cyber attacks against corporate networks by 50% between 2020 and 2021, according to research from Check Point. The increased demand for defense has caused an acute talent shortage: while many other industries were laying people off, cybersecurity teams and vendors were struggling to find experienced professionals to help harden companies' defenses.

It is well-known that cybersecurity spending, even in times of economic uncertainty, does not typically trend backward. When times are bad, cyber criminal activity does not slow down. The year 2022 is the most recent example of that: the number of cyber attacks went up, and while budgets were frozen, only a few organizations made cuts in their security teams. To put it simply: nobody wants to take responsibility and say "I think we can cut our security spending".

The fact that security has been seen as an almost certain way for investors to make money has led to an oversupply of capital. Many VC firms, solo general partners (GPs), and even family offices wanted to get exposure to cybersecurity because it was seen as a "hot market". But, since few of them had the expertise and the network to evaluate security companies, many unscrupulous founders were able to raise capital without solving a real market problem, and sometimes without any idea of what they were going to do.

The continuous flow of capital and the VC craze of 2021-2022 greatly slowed down the process of natural selection where only good startups could get funding to grow, resulting in a market flooded with tools of questionable value. Over time, this imbalance will correct itself, and it is likely to be a painful process for many startups in the field.

There is a lot of siloed thinking and reinventing the wheel

Although many people come into security from other walks of life, few retain the ability to see the industry in a broader context, not as an isolated, self-contained field. This has two important implications.

First, those working in the security industry often assume that the problems and trends seen in security are unique. Take the number of vendors: people often complain that "there are just too many vendors - we don't need so many tools doing the same thing". Although that may very well be true, this problem is not specific to the security industry: e.g. in human resources (HR) tech space alone, there are over 21,000 vendors while the financial technology (fintech) space features over 30,000 competing companies. Terms and trends such as the so-called industry consolidation aren't a security invention either, but a dynamic that shapes virtually all areas of business, and is often referred to as "bundling and unbundling".

The second implication of security professionals having a limited view into other fields is they don't benefit from the accumulated knowledgebase in the more mature areas of technology. The discipline of software engineering, for example, has developed continuous automated testing, continuous deployment and integration, version control, and other tools and approaches that can successfully be adopted in cybersecurity. Instead of looking outwards and borrowing concepts that have been well-understood by professionals in other fields, security is constantly choosing a hard path of intellectual independence, trying to reinvent the wheel and find its own answers. Naturally, this comes at a cost without necessarily leading to great results.

Small supply of talent and a large number of serial founders

To start a cybersecurity company, one generally needs to have a solid, hands-on experience in the field. As the industry itself is new, deeply technical, and fast-changing, the pool of people capable of identifying and successfully tackling a well-defined problem area is relatively small. Cybersecurity is not something most people can accidentally get exposed to, quickly see an opportunity, and act on it. It is most certainly not a field where passionate university students get a shot at building a unicorn.

While the supply of technical talent is small, the percentage of people who are entrepreneurial in addition to being technical is even smaller. Despite growing demand and the readiness of VCs to pour capital into the field, there are not a lot of practitioners who can build a cybersecurity company. Moreover, high compensation packages offered to security practitioners in the US do not create incentives for people to take risks and launch their own ventures.

Since so much of the industry is based on relationships, and B2B enterprise sales are about working with a small number of CISOs, a first-time founder who builds relationships with a good number of security leaders, will find that building a second company is much easier, regardless of the outcome of their first venture. That is why it is common to see repeat entrepreneurs with a strong track of success in cybersecurity.

Expert Insight

"Our industry has experienced multiple boom and bust cycles, influenced by many factors that Ross has outlined. However, compared to the broader technology sector, cybersecurity has consistently been more stable. This stability is reflected in the overall budgets, which predictably grow each year, aligning with inflation and the growth in IT spending.

This trend is due to cybersecurity's inherent focus on leading-edge risks, driven by rapid technological evolution, and unknown threats, stemming from offensive cybersecurity tactics. In nearly every economic scenario, cybersecurity budgets are among the last to be reduced in financially healthy organizations. A common saying exemplifies this priority: 'While I can trim my IT budget, there's no way I'll tell my board that we need to scale back on cybersecurity.'"

- William Lin, Co-Founder and CEO of AKA Identity, Co-Creator and Board Chairman of Security Tinkerers, previously Founding Partner and Managing Director at Forgepoint Capital

SECTION 2

Understanding the cybersecurity ecosystem

Investors

To grow, cybersecurity startups need capital. In some fields, founders are dealing with less technologically sophisticated buyers, so they can stitch something together using no-code or low-code tools, and get an enterprise prospect to do a proof of value (POV) of the solution. That is not at all the case in B2B, enterprise-focused security: no security team will bother testing a product that it cannot potentially implement. Now, it doesn't mean that prototypes aren't valuable - they very much are, as they help founders explain their idea to investors and prospects at the pre-product stage. This also doesn't mean that a beta version of the new product needs to be fully enterprise-ready for someone from the security team to test it in a non-production environment. However, the reality is that there needs to be a minimally viable product, and to build it, the startup must invest in research and development (R&D), which requires access to capital.

Some companies find a way to fully bootstrap their operations. South Africa-based Thinkst Canary is one of them - the company has grown to over $10 million in annual recurring revenue (ARR) without raising any investment. While that's a great example, the reality is that for many, not taking any external capital may not be the most prudent option, especially if they want to grow their business fast.

I will share some thoughts about fundraising later in this book. This section provides an overview of suppliers of capital - angel investors, angel networks and syndicates, and venture firms. I will discuss cybersecurity accelerators and incubators even though their role goes beyond providing funding. It is worth noting that there are many funding options that are not covered in this book. The financial instruments startups have access to can be complicated, especially at the later stages of the company. There are private equity (PE) investors, venture-debt lenders, and other entities that I won't be talking about here.

Additionally, I am not going to be looking at non-dilutive government grants. My stance is that while some countries provide "free" money options that do not reduce founders' ownership in their companies, I don't believe grants should be considered as a good source of capital for product startups. This is because applying for grants, and later, reporting about the usage of funds, are typically complicated and bureaucratic processes that consume limited time and resources. Most founders are better off by focusing on their customers, solving problems someone is willing to pay for, designing business models that help them achieve goals, and raising growth capital when, if, and as much as needed. People's circumstances may vary, but in my world (B2B enterprise-focused companies serving the US market), an hour spent on filling out government forms is an hour not spent on building and selling software, and therefore an hour wasted.

Angel investors

Angel investors: fundamentals

Angel investors are individuals: security leaders, security practitioners, owners of security service providers, entrepreneurs, and others who invest their own money in startups. Angel checks are small, anywhere between $5,000 and $100,000 although the actual amounts vary widely.

Angel investors are the people willing to support entrepreneurs at the earliest stage of their journeys, when there is just an early prototype, wireframes, a beta version of the product, or sometimes nothing but a slide deck with an idea. Unlike VCs, they don't typically get to invest full-time, but that doesn't mean they are less helpful. I have met many angels who spend countless hours outside of work trying to set their portfolio companies up for success.

Two other factors make angels different from VCs and other types of investors. First, they typically invest via a SAFE note. SAFE stands for Simple Agreement for Future Equity and describes an arrangement where startups receive money from an investor when the deal closes, but angels don't immediately get shares in the company. Instead, their investment converts into equity in the startup at some point in the future, typically during the priced round, when VCs come into the picture. This removes the need to determine valuation and negotiate legal terms upfront, greatly simplifying the transaction for both founders and investors.

The second factor that makes angels rather unique is that they sometimes exit their investments before anyone else, such as VCs. They do it by selling their ownership in the company to venture firms at later stages of the company lifecycle, typically at Series A or beyond. If the startup is doing well, VCs that participate in one of the subsequent funding rounds are happy to increase their stake by purchasing shares from early angels at a discount - often in a process called "tender offer". As a side effect, the capitalization table of the company (the document that lists all the investors and their ownership stake) gets shorter, or as people in the industry say, "cleaner", making it easier to manage.

Types of angel investors and their motivations

Different angels in the cybersecurity industry are motivated by different factors. Broadly, there are two kinds of angel investors: active and passive. Active angels are looking to get hands-on, supporting founders on their journey to build a company. Passive angels, on the other hand, see themselves as suppliers of capital. They are not interested in getting their hands dirty; instead, their goal is to write a check and let founders do what they set out to do.

There is no right or wrong approach here, and what makes sense in the specific circumstances is highly contextual. A serial entrepreneur who knows what they are doing may benefit from having passive angels on board who let them execute their vision and don't distract them with questions and ideas. On the other hand, a first-time founder with little experience building a company may be better served by getting active angels to help and fill in the gaps in their knowledge. Founders and angels must be transparent about their desires and ways in which they are looking to be involved; it is the lack of such transparency and unmet expectations that lead to conflicts and damage relationships.

The non-financial motivations that get people into investing vary widely. Some CISOs and security practitioners see angel investing as a way to stay on top of the new developments in the industry and influence the product direction of the next generation of path-defining companies. This desire to be plugged into the ecosystem is often a defining factor that keeps angels actively engaged in the space. For many, especially security entrepreneurs with prior exits, investing is a way to give back and support the next generation of founders. A founder who successfully exited a cybersecurity company may decide to allocate some of their own capital to help others build startups they believe should exist in the industry. I have also met several people who started angel investing so that they can build a track record and later transition into the VC space as partners or even raise their own funds. Sourcing deals, going through the investment memos, and getting familiar with the due diligence process can be a great way to build the investing muscles and decide if venture capital is something that could be interesting as a full-time career.

The ability to generate financial returns can also be a good motivator for people who choose to invest in cybersecurity startups. In my opinion, however, money is by far the worst reason to angel invest: most early-stage ventures fail, and it's no secret that unless one goes deep into it, and builds a diversified portfolio of companies, they are unlikely to make substantial returns. The stories about people striking it big by becoming early investors in Google or Uber suffer from survivorship bias, similar to those about lottery winners. Although the vast majority of those who play the lottery lose, we only get to read the interviews with winners.

Some angels are brought in because of their "brand value" which can help founders secure funding from VCs. These investors are easy to recognize as they are prominent on fundraising decks: former CISOs of companies that had large exits, co-founders of well-known enterprises, or CFOs of widely recognized technology leaders. On the other hand, angels such as doctors and dentists that have the money to invest, but may require a lot of hand-holding and reporting because they're new to SaaS can be considered "low value" to cybersecurity founders.

Expert Insight

"There is a second facet to characterizing the type of angel investor; those that invest in the unique innovation of the technology vs. the experience of the executive team. The argument for investing in the innovative nature of the technology is that the product will sell itself, since it should be obvious to a customer that it solves some problem. The angel that looks for an experienced executive team realizes that for many types of products, the technology is not enough, and experience in the funding, development, marketing, sales, and hiring processes is the key to building a company. This type of team can pivot the technology to meet the market. Both investment approaches have merit."

- Steve Zalewski, startup advisor and angel investor, previously CISO at Levi Strauss & Co.

Value-add of angel investors

When an angel gets involved with an early-stage company, there is little that can be formally evaluated, quantified, and analyzed: there is no product, no customers, often no employees, and sometimes, even no legal entity. The whole startup may very well be a great idea and two or three passionate people are crazy enough to believe they can make it happen but with little experience in what it will take to get there. For the startup to be able to raise growth capital from VCs and scale its operations, it needs to get to a level that is significantly more advanced. It needs strong, provable signals of customer demand, ideally a functional product, and a strong team of early employees with relevant experience that can convince VCs they can pull it off. Moreover, the company needs to be legally incorporated and present a variety of documents during due diligence, from vesting agreements between founders to balance sheet and cap table.

The single most important job of an angel investor is to help the company get to the next stage and raise growth funding from VCs. To accomplish this goal, angels should be able, among other things:

- Help startups validate their problem space by making introductions to the experts in the field and pointing founders to the right resources.
- Help startups build and test the early version of the solution by becoming or introducing founders to prospective early customers, or making connections to potential design partners.
- Help founders craft a winning fundraising strategy, coach them about pitching to VCs, and make introductions to investors.
- Help companies define and test different go-to-market strategies so that they can do more of what works and less of what doesn't, and accumulate enough valuable learnings to scale without wasting more resources than what's required.
- Help entrepreneurs hit the right milestones that VCs will need to build conviction and ultimately write a check on good terms.

Angels are connectors, and since their main role is to help the company reach the next milestone, they are greatly incentivized to support founders. One way through which they do it is by making introductions to VCs and other angels. Venture capital firms rely on angel investors to incubate the next generation of high-growth companies, and help them get discovered by VCs. It's a win-win for everyone involved: founders get warm introductions to the most reputable investors, angels get to see the value of their stake in the company grow, and VCs get access to the best early-stage deals.

Working with angels

For experienced security leaders and practitioners, the easiest way to get on the radar of angel investors is to privately reach out to people in their network with whom they have good relationships through past work, industry affiliations, and the like. When angels decide to back a startup, they base their decisions first and foremost on their belief that the founding team can turn its vision into reality.

Best founders know that the real value-add of angels doesn't come from capital; it comes from the resources and help they are willing to provide. Most angels are truly passionate about the industry - they are CISOs, security practitioners, and entrepreneurs who want to fund companies they believe should exist in security. Experienced founders know that angels are doing what they do as a hobby, so they keep them informed about company progress, formulate specific asks, and make it easy for angels to provide help. Moreover, even if a funding round is led by a large VC, smart entrepreneurs will always reserve a small allocation for angels they would like to get on board.

Expert Insight

"When evaluating an opportunity, angel investors are first and foremost looking for the three T's: team, timing, and traction; each one is important, and altogether they give confidence in an early-stage deal. The ideal team is experienced (in the best case, has multiple exits), knows their market, and can tell you the weakness of any player in the market - especially market incumbent. Timing is all about ensuring the customers are ready to consume the technology - catching the wave of a new technology or new market requirement. Being too early often results in the same outcome as being too late. Traction can come in many forms - open source, early design partners, or even

customers. If there are paying customers and the team has navigated sophisticated procurement processes, that's a great sign.

Most early-stage security companies fail because they can't identify champions that care enough about their product or idea (aka failure to find product-market fit) or because their product is too complex for champions to procure. While the solution the company has built might be addressing a real problem, if the problem is shared by multiple owners in a typical organization, there simply might not be any budget allocated to solving it. Similarly, if no project exists to solve the problem, and thus, it's a problem that falls to the wayside, or existing solutions are seen as 'good enough', no deal is going to get pushed through procurement. Some investors describe this by saying that a new technology needs to be 10x better than the existing solution.

A close secondary to the three T's which fundamentally is just another way to look at the team and their ability to execute in the early stage, is investigating and evaluating their product discovery process. Sophisticated teams will have already interviewed many security practitioners, often prompting them with nothing more than 'We're thinking of focusing on this problem' and listening to what they say. The more sophisticated the product discovery process, and the more committed the founders are to getting out of the way of customer insight, the more likely they are to succeed."

- Jonathan Cran, angel investor at Resilient Thesis, previously Founder and CEO at Intrigue

Expert Insight

"Don't forget to check for founder-angel fit as well. Different angels come with different areas of expertise, but you are looking for somebody passionate about the problem you are solving. A good way to check if it's a fit is by asking yourself if you would hire that person. Great angels are going through the trenches with you, are a call away - and not just commenting something obvious on your quarterly update."

- Robert Kugler, angel investor and a member of the Cyber Club London (CCL)

Angel syndicates and angel networks

Angel syndicates: fundamentals

Angel syndicates are formal groups of angels who pull capital and make investments together.

Traditionally, every angel was responsible for finding their own deals, convincing founders to take the money from them and not someone else, evaluating companies, and supporting their portfolio investments. Moreover, angels needed to be willing to write checks at a certain minimum dollar amount, be it $20,000 or $50,000. Taking smaller amounts created unnecessary troubles for the founders because each investor needed to be recorded on their capitalization (cap) table, a document that captures everyone who owns shares in the company. When the company needed to have all investors sign a document, founders were forced to chase people down even though the amount they invested was often insignificant. Additionally, dealing with tens of investors creates significant overhead; everyone has questions, opinions, and perspectives, and wants to share them, diverting the founder's attention away from building the business. For angels who were willing to support an entrepreneur but unable to commit to certain minimum investment amounts, the inability to participate in the company's success was upsetting.

Angel syndicates emerged as a way to democratize angel investing and address many of these challenges for both founders and investors. Specifically, they made it possible for entrepreneurs to accept smaller checks from tens or even hundreds of angels without having to convince every single one of them separately, deal with hundreds of separate payments, and investor updates. Moreover, regardless of how many people invested via a syndicate, only the syndicate itself, not everyone who put in their money, would appear on the cap table, and only one person, a syndicate lead, would need to sign papers and make decisions on behalf of all syndicate investors.

For angels, syndicates greatly lowered the barriers to investing. Not only do they provide steady deal flow, and leverage the power of the community to conduct due diligence, but they also lower the amount an individual needs to put in per deal to as little as $2,000 or $5,000.

Mechanics of the angel syndicate model

Every syndicate conducts business in a slightly different way: some are invite-only while others are open to any accredited investor; some have unique restrictions about who can become a member (e.g. CISO-only), and others are more flexible.

Syndicates consist of a lead or a group of leads and members or individual investors (at a cyber-focused syndicate they could be security practitioners, CISOs, and experienced security entrepreneurs). A large syndicate may have formal "committees", working groups of people responsible for certain aspects of the work such as legal, marketing, operations, due diligence, etc.

When a member, lead, or committee brings a company for consideration, a dedicated due diligence group is formed from relevant people to assess the startup and decide if the syndicate will invest. If the decision is positive, the lead will negotiate an allocation with the founder (the amount of money the startup is willing to accept from the group), put in some of their own money, and make the rest of the allotment available for other members to invest. Each member is free to review the pitch deck and the investment memo prepared by the due diligence committee and attend a Q&A session with the founder organized for the whole group.

The organizers of the syndicate, often called leads, typically do all the upfront work of meeting founders, sourcing and evaluating startups, negotiating an allocation, writing investment memos, pitching the deal to the members, collecting payments, and distributing post-investment updates at no cost. As compensation for all the efforts, when and if the deal is successful and the syndicate exits, it usually takes 10-20% of the profits. This way, everyone's interests are aligned: if the investment is not successful, everyone including the leads loses their money; if it is, the leads get rewarded for all the work.

Unlike VCs, angel syndicates don't raise money upfront, and don't charge management fees. The capital collected minus the fees of platforms such as AngelList used to manage the whole process and handle legal, accounting, and annual reporting, goes directly to the portfolio company.

Advantages and disadvantages of working with angel syndicates

For cybersecurity startup founders, the advantages of working with syndicates include:

- A chance to work with domain experts who can understand in detail what the startup is trying to do, what problem it is tackling, and whether the proposed solution is feasible.
- Ability to get funding from potential customers and security practitioners with deep connections in the industry and a strong passion for supporting the products they believe in.
- Building relationships with security professionals who are active in the ecosystem and can spread the word about the startup's mission. Angel investors are often leaders in their communities, speakers at events and conferences, advisors to early-stage ventures, organizers of Capture the Flag competitions, and the like.

- An opportunity to get different forms of support, including advice from experienced practitioners, product feedback, and help with the go-to-market strategy, something traditional investors may not be as well positioned to provide.
- Because angels invest their own money, they do not have a set time horizon, unlike VCs who need to exit all of their investments within 10 years. However, this varies greatly. Some angels are long-term players, and their strategic focus makes them very unlikely to push startups into the growth patterns that founders are not interested in pursuing. Others, on the other hand, do angel investing precisely because the time to exit for angels is fast, so they are looking to see the returns quickly.
- By working with syndicates, founders can tap into a broad network of people and get money from a large and diverse collective of supporters. At the same time, they benefit from only having one line on the cap table, a very important factor for anyone planning to raise subsequent rounds of funding. This is why whenever founders are approached by friends and relatives looking to put in some cash in their companies, those thinking long-term often encourage them to invest via syndicates.

Fundamentally, angel syndicates enable founders to reach a large number of angels in one place, greatly simplifying a way to get investment and opening new networks for people who do not have many connections in the industry. When it comes to security-focused syndicates, it's worth noting that there are very few of them: one or two in Europe, and just under five in the US. In Israel, angel networks are so well-developed that there is much less need for a formalized syndicate structure.

Although angel syndicates can be great partners for cybersecurity startups, they are not always the best solution. This is the case for several reasons.

While angel syndicates that bring together security practitioners and leaders are great for early-stage ventures, they are typically not a good fit for companies further in the lifecycle. The average check size of angel syndicates is somewhere between $50,000 and $250,000, well below what an established later-stage company would need to supercharge its growth. Having said that, angel syndicates are typically well-connected and have established relationships with VCs, so they can be of great help when their portfolio companies are looking to raise the next rounds of funding.

The biggest potential downside of working with a syndicate is the fact that the number of people who will see the pitch deck is higher than in a regular VC. This is not surprising: a typical syndicate would have 50+ members, compared to a VC firm where the number of associates and partners who will go through the deck is typically below ten. While most angel syndicates take the matters of confidentiality seriously and vet their members, and platforms like AngelList have strong measures in place to prevent the leakage of data, the fact remains that syndicates involve more people hence why they are more likely to expose a pitch deck to those it wasn't intended for. Although a large community is one of the key assets that enable syndicates to evangelize the startup's mission and make potential connections to customers, it can also have downsides for those in stealth mode. The best way to lower the risks is to openly discuss the concerns with the syndicate lead and see what they say.

Angel investment networks

Angel networks are communities of investors who come together to learn, network, share experiences, and deal flow, help one another with due diligence, and otherwise support each other on their investment journey. Unlike angel syndicates, investment networks do not pull the capital together, which means that the usual minimum investment requirements for individual angels will still apply. Angel networks are good places for companies to find investment between their angel rounds, which are often pre-revenue and pre-MVP, and their first institutional round, which is often somewhere between pre-seed and seed.

Expert Insight

"It is important to understand that not all angel investors are created equal.

Angels who also happen to be domain experts and super connectors are worth their weight in gold. When you are raising capital from individual angels, you get to work with one or two people, but with angel syndicates, you are creating an army of friends, supporters, and cheerleaders who will boost your morale every step of the way with all the highs and lows that the startup experience has to offer.

When you are getting investments from angel syndicates, you get advisors for the life of the company and not just the industry standard two-year advisory agreements. Moreover, although not everyone in the syndicate might invest in a particular startup deal, after the investment, a startup becomes a portfolio company of the whole group and has access to other angels in the syndicate which is literally a 'buy one get one' deal for a startup.

Getting investment from a well-known angel syndicate that performs technical due diligence also provides a great signal to follow-on investors. It tells them that if well-known security leaders are willing to put their own money into a startup after thorough due diligence, there must be something unique they saw. Startups that have raised money from such syndicates have often done well in their next funding rounds raising at healthy multiples."

- Anshu Gupta, CISO and angel investor, member of Silicon Valley CISO Investments

Startup incubators, accelerators, and venture studios

Startup incubators and accelerators: fundamentals

Startup incubators and accelerators provide early-stage ventures with a small amount of funding, combined with comprehensive programming directed at launching or scaling a company or achieving a major milestone. The process of getting accepted into an accelerator is competitive. Selected companies receive mentorship, introductions to industry experts and potential customers, as well as access to other resources. Although there are some differences between how accelerators and incubators operate and add value to the ecosystem, for simplicity I will be using these two terms interchangeably.

Startup accelerators and incubators have different sources of capital and business models. Some are funded by universities or various levels of government, some are run by venture funds, while others are financed by corporate sponsorships or by charging program fees to participants. In exchange for their support, accelerators and incubators that are run as for-profit organizations usually take a small ownership stake in the company, about 5-10% on average.

Value-add of incubators and accelerators

For first-time founders and those who haven't yet had the chance to scale a company from a few people to millions in ARR, startup accelerators and incubators can make a huge difference. This is especially the case in cybersecurity where technical founders often lack the experience doing what it takes to build a business - defining the go-to-market strategy, handling fundraising, hiring, operations, and other areas critical to business success.

The value of participating in cyber-focused accelerators and incubators differs from the value of industry-agnostic programs.

Security is a nuanced space, and those without a deep understanding of these nuances typically find it hard to navigate the industry.

Building products in security requires founders and product teams to design their solutions while considering the new threats that may emerge six months from the time they release a minimum viable product (MVP). Recruitment requires one to remember the talent shortage and the need to grow the talent internally while recognizing that the threat landscape is going to evolve, and with that so will the skills people must develop to remain successful at what they do. Marketing in cybersecurity has a unique flavor because of the strong reliance on trust in purchasing decisions. Even the way storytelling works in security is different from other industries, as there is always a big educational component to it: you can't sell security without educating your customers about the need to buy your product.

Cyber-focused startup accelerators and incubators help founders expand their networks in a short period, meeting potential customers, security leaders, technical partners, and fellow entrepreneurs. For an early-stage venture, being able to get an introduction to tens of CISOs can be a game changer: a conversation that starts from the angle of "a founder looking to learn" is typically much more productive compared to those that take the "founder looking to sell" route.

On the flip side, accelerators and incubators not focused on specific domains tend to view the world in simpler and broader ways, and the fact that they don't know all the nuances of cybersecurity can open them to new angles and bring new ideas to the table. Moreover, industry-agnostic organizations have seen what works and what doesn't across different sectors, so startups trying to disrupt the way security is delivered or founders who already have strong networks in their field and are looking for new perspectives may find them more useful.

Expert Insight

"It is clear that first-time founders, by definition, have not yet developed the skills enjoyed by experienced entrepreneurs. In spite of that lack of experience, accelerators and incubators can definitely help founders leverage proven frameworks to better interpret market signals, evaluate

good (or bad) options, strategically and financially plan, and identify shortcuts to de-risk opportunities quickly. But, what might be understated is how essential these frameworks are to communicating a vision for a technology business that is familiar to investors. Accelerators and incubators are good at imbuing their founders with these skills."

- Rick Gordon, Co-Founder and CEO at Tidal Cyber

Deciding whether to join incubators and accelerators

Founders trying to decide if it's worth participating in an accelerator or an incubator should start by doing the gap analysis: assessing where they are, where they are looking to get, and what they need to get there. The cost of participation is another factor worth taking into account. While some government-funded programs can be free, most quality accelerators take a percentage of the company equity in exchange for programming and a small check or charge a program fee. Lastly, entrepreneurs should assess what resources they already have or can access in other places. For example, established VC firms would typically have someone responsible for supporting their portfolio companies, helping with hiring, and making introductions. Getting backed by a top-tier venture firm can eliminate the need to look for help elsewhere. Israeli VCs go even further, often providing founders with hands-on help around sales, defining the go-to-market strategy, establishing partnerships, managing engineering, building products, and more.

Confident and experienced operators with all the necessary skills to build a company, or people who have just left a fast-growing startup where they played an active role in building it from the ground up, can likely build a business on their own. Founding teams that lack expertise in running a company and don't have people in their network who can help, would often benefit from support around product, go-to-market strategy, hiring, operations, fundraising, and the like. For them, joining an industry-agnostic or a cyber-focused accelerator could be a good idea, but certainly not a necessity. Access to knowledge and experience has been greatly democratized, and security practitioners with an ambition to build great companies can find the information they need, and even mentors and supporters, without having to give away a chunk of their business or pay thousands of dollars in fees.

The top-tier startup accelerators deserve a separate mention. Historically, being accepted to the highly selective, exclusive cohort run by one of the few leading accelerators signaled to the market, namely the investors, media, and early customers that the company has a great future and is worth looking at. The value of signaling has been going down in recent years, as these accelerators greatly expanded their reach and started accepting hundreds of startups to each cohort, diluting the experience participants receive. Some founders come to accelerators because they are looking for structured programs to help them reach the next milestone. While there is value in that, and accelerators that get their cohort companies to work hard and make great progress for the demo day can indeed make a big difference in the company's trajectory, I think founders should be well capable of maintaining focus on what matters even without being a part of a structured, fast-track program. Building a company requires years of hard work, so entrepreneurs will be better served by developing the skills needed to control their focus and velocity without relying on external parties to do it for them.

Some accelerators actively encourage cohort participants and alumni to buy products and services from one another, thus creating a closed mini-economy. If the ideal customer profile (ICP) of a security company is an early-stage startup, then taking part in the program could unlock new distribution channels and be well worth the cost. The flipside of this is that selling only to "friendlies" can give startups a false sense of the product-market fit because they never actually validate their ideal customer profile. Startups in accelerators that encourage mutual support want to show "traction" so they sell to other friendly startups, but hit a wall when they try to sell outside of the cohort and end up going back to the drawing board.

It is worth adding a warning against the so-called serial accelerator participation. In the past decade, as we have seen the popularization of startups, it became common for founders to jump from one accelerator to another in the hope of getting access to more useful resources. While joining a startup incubator or accelerator can give founders valuable support, the perceived safety net is not real: to succeed, they still need to hustle, find customers, and do the work. Moving from one accelerator to another can feel like progress, but all it is doing is taking away the time and attention from pursuing the goals that matter.

Lastly, founders need to be careful about the amount of equity they are giving away. Some accelerators take as much as 15 or 20% in exchange for very little cash, which can create problems down the line when companies go to raise a proper seed from VCs. Many early-stage VCs target 15-20% ownership to make their fund dynamics work, and an accelerator with high ownership can make deals prohibitive for those VCs.

A brief look at the venture studio model

The venture studio model is much more hands-on and is different from an accelerator or an incubator, focusing on building one to five companies per year instead of making bets on many. People running a venture studio find and validate ideas, estimate opportunity size, and assess what it will take to succeed. If the business model, risks, and economics make sense, they hire founders to turn the idea into reality. Founders are paid a salary sufficient to cover their basic expenses and receive a meaningful portion of equity so that they are motivated to make the startup a success. Those running a venture studio act like co-founders rather than passive investors, especially at the early stages of the company. They do a lot of the work to de-risk the new venture and offer hands-on support around product development, sales, roadmapping, recruitment, and so on.

To make the economics of this model work, venture studios need to take a bigger chunk of the cap table early in the company's lifecycle: it is not uncommon for them to own 35-50% of the startup. Such a high percentage of the ownership is justified because the studio takes the risks, pays the founders a salary, and does a lot of the early work.

Not all venture studios are created equal. Some do a lot of the heavy lifting and have arrangements with VCs in their networks who are ready to provide additional growth funding on founder-friendly terms. Others offer little value but take unreasonably large amounts of equity which can cause problems for their own company's future and its ability to raise capital. When the startup is going for a seed round, and founders already only own 20-30% of the company, it is clear that their motivation for making it a success is not going to be as high.

Venture studios are appropriate for mature, sophisticated ecosystems with well-developed talent such as San Francisco and Washington, D.C. in the US and Tel Aviv in Israel. For a first-time founder who doesn't have an idea they are passionate about or a strong co-founder but who is capable of executing, venture studios can be a great way to get started. For experienced entrepreneurs and those with a good idea, solid co-founders, and strong networks in the industry, this may be a costly way forward.

Expert Insight

"Building a startup is a lot like dancing in the middle of a minefield in the middle of the night: the chances of getting through intact are remote unless you have a map. Of course, not all maps are created equal. Similarly, not all incubators, accelerators, or venture studios are created equal. Incubators are more akin to crib notes whereas venture studios more closely resemble partners. Both have their places but are materially different. Entrepreneurs should be interested in the results, the proof points, and the degree to which startup success can be attributed to an incubator or a studio the company participated in. Cyber entrepreneurs without prior startup experience need all the help and support they can get."

- Bob Ackerman, Founder and Managing Director at AllegisCyber Capital and Co-Founder of DataTribe

Deep Dive

To learn more about the accelerator and incubator business models, and what makes it challenging to run them, check out a Venture in Security deep dive titled "The tough business of incubating cyber innovation: a deep look at the cybersecurity-focused incubator and accelerator models". You can find it by navigating to https://ventureinsecurity.net/p/the-tough-business-of-incubating or by scanning this QR code.

Venture capital firms

Venture capital firms: fundamentals

Venture capital (VC) firms provide entrepreneurs, including those in cybersecurity, with growth capital in exchange for equity or ownership in the company. Startups are high-risk ventures that require money for growth but have no valuable assets to offer as collateral. Since the traditional financial institutions were unable to serve these needs, the VC space emerged as a response to the market gap.

The VC model relies on the power law - the principle according to which a single investment will yield returns which are orders of magnitude larger than all other investments combined. Since investments in startups are risky, most bets will fail. Those that succeed, have to make it big yielding multiples of 5x-100x or more to not only pay for the losses but also to generate profit. This explains the expectations that the company that receives funding will attempt to grow quickly and a lot. The so-called "triple, triple, double, double, double" rule which refers to tripling & doubling the revenue every year in the first five years is the direct outcome of this model.

Venture capital firms: the model

VC firms solve two problems. For institutions that hold large amounts of capital such as pension funds, sovereign wealth funds, and endowments, as well as high-net-worth individuals, they offer an opportunity to diversify their portfolio into high-risk assets. For startup founders, VCs provide growth capital on easy-to-understand and easy-to-fulfill conditions, in exchange for a percentage ownership in the company.

Investors who put their money into the VC fund are called Limited Partners or LPs. When a specified amount of money is raised, it forms a fund - a portion of capital that has to be allocated within the first 3-5 years and returned to LPs after a decade (although in real life, the average fund age is closer to 12-13 years). Although VCs do not invest their own capital, people running VC funds (called General Partners) are expected to put in a bit of their money so that they are financially aligned & motivated to do well.

General Partners of the fund get paid in two ways. First, they receive a percentage of the fund's profits, commonly referred to as "carried interest" or "carry". After the fund is liquidated, the LPs will first get their money back, then they get what's called a "hurdle rate", a guaranteed interest income or the amount of money they would get if they were to keep their capital elsewhere for that decade. The remaining amount which constitutes profits is split between the LPs and GPs on the 80/20 basis: VCs get 20%, and the investors in the fund get 80%.

Another way VCs get compensated for their work is by using the 2% of the fund size as a "management fee" to cover operating expenses of the fund which includes rent, travel, office expenses, events, as well as salaries and bonuses of partners and employees.

Incentives of the VC firms

The ways VCs get paid inform what they are incentivized to do.

The expectation that venture capital firms will return the fund and generate profits for their LPs, and the implications of the previously mentioned power law means that companies that are more likely to get the money are looking to grow fast, have the team positioned to succeed and tackle a problem that has a large total addressable market (TAM).

The fact that VC funds get to spend 2% of the fund size on operating expenses, salaries, and bonuses, has been motivating investors to raise bigger funds. The math is simple: the bigger the fund, the bigger the dollar value of the 2% and the more money the VC can spend every year. For founders, bigger funds often mean bigger check sizes and higher valuations because the amount of money the VC invests, the company valuation, and the amount of equity investors will own after the transaction is complete are all linked together.

Expert Insight

"While it is true that often, bigger funds lead to bigger check sizes, this is not always the case. A $100M fund and a $1B fund might invest roughly the same check size and for roughly the same valuation at seed. Funds can be constructed in many ways. A bigger fund might invest across early and growth stages, and/or they might keep reserves in the fund in order to participate in follow-on fundings for their early-stage companies. A bigger fund might also have different expectations around outcomes. An important nuance more founders need to understand is that the dynamics of returning a $100M fund are different from the dynamics of returning a $1B fund. Bigger funds need homerun, multi-billion exit outcomes to work, whereas a $100M fund VC that owns 20% of its portfolio companies could return the fund with one $500M acquisition."

- Allison Averill, Vice President at Unusual Ventures

Types of VC firms investing in cybersecurity

Although there are different ways to slice and dice the investor landscape, fundamentally there are two types of VCs who fund cybersecurity innovation:

- Specialist VCs - VC firms whose mandate is to invest exclusively or predominantly in cybersecurity companies.
- Generalist VCs - VC firms whose mandate is to invest in companies from different industries, not just those in cybersecurity although they may have partners fully or partially dedicated to security.

Advantages and disadvantages of cyber-focused VC funds

Deep domain expertise enables cyber-focused VC firms to attract founders and efficiently evaluate potential investments. VC firms that exclusively invest in cybersecurity see substantially more security companies compared to the generalist VCs. This naturally equips them with the ability to spot patterns, and therefore quickly and efficiently assess the idea, the founding team, the go-to-market, and even the tech stack of the company, and compare them to those of other startups they have been seeing. Since cybersecurity is such a complex technical field, it's not uncommon for founders to get frustrated when a generalist VC asks them questions that appear to be basic and reveal their low familiarity with the domain which doesn't happen as often with experienced security investors.

Security is an industry heavily reliant on trust, and early-stage startups often struggle to get any attention from decision-makers in the field. Cyber-focused VCs tend to have strong networks in cybersecurity which enables them to do deeper due diligence on potential investments, and most importantly, help their portfolio companies with introductions to design partners, resellers, and early customers.

Sector specialization, however, comes with its own downsides. Cybersecurity lives in the broader context of trends and ideas that shape other fields, be it the consumerization of user experience in B2B enterprise SaaS, bottom-up adoption of new products in the field of developer tooling, everything-as-code approaches in IT infrastructure, the adoption of DevOps, or the rise of no-code in marketing. Being fully focused on security makes it likely that the firm will lose a broader view of the tech market, and fail to anticipate how emerging trends in other fields can reshape cybersecurity. Additionally, all industries are cyclical, and focusing exclusively on one market segment may make it hard for investors to adjust when the trends reverse. Although so far cybersecurity has mostly enjoyed continued growth or at the very least some level of stability, it is unlikely to be the case forever. When the trends change, cyber-focused VCs may struggle to remain relevant, raise new funds, and continue supporting their founders.

Advantages and disadvantages of generalist VC funds

Generalist VCs that invest in cybersecurity range from firms that do not have any understanding of security to those that have strong expertise in the field. The latter, which includes top-tier and large VCs, often have partners fully or partially dedicated to security. A large number of firms fall somewhere in between these two extremes: some may have partners interested in security but who are not able to allocate much time to it, while others may hire principals or senior associates with domain experience to help source and evaluate companies in fields where managing partners themselves do not possess the right expertise.

The exposure to different markets and market segments, and subsequently, different ideas, perspectives, and approaches, enable generalist VCs to think about the broad range of potential outcomes and industry development paths. Because cybersecurity exists within the context of the larger tech ecosystem, the ability to observe the dynamics in IT, infrastructure software, developer tooling, deep tech, and various segments of the B2B SaaS, is highly beneficial if one wants to bet on high-risk, and potentially high-reward, industry-defining innovations.

Generalist VCs have a larger pool of potential investment options, as they are choosing the best company from a broad list of companies, not the best cybersecurity company from a much smaller pool of security startups. Furthermore, the fact that industry-agnostic VCs are not beholden to the destiny of any one single market segment, means that they are much more likely to ensure their own long-term survival.

The weak sides of generalist VCs include a lack of domain expertise and market awareness in security. The investor may not understand many of the nuances surrounding building cybersecurity companies such as high reliance on trust and its implications, the long buying cycles and the role of industry analysts, and the complexity of conducting customer research. Without such understanding, it can be hard to add value post-investment, especially at the earlier stages when founders need some guidance and support to get the product to the market and get to the product-market fit quickly.

Generalist VC firms with expertise in cybersecurity are, in my opinion, the best of both worlds. Investors in generalist funds maintain their ability to get insights from other verticals and horizontals, understand trends shaping a broader range of markets, and develop well-rounded perspectives about the tech scene. At the same time, they have strong domain expertise and networks in cybersecurity, making it possible to imagine what can work in the industry.

Making sense of the complexity of the VC space

Founders looking to raise venture capital must first and foremost understand how the VC model works. VCs aren't there to transform the future of technology, or advance a specific industry: they are professional investors hired by those with capital (Limited Partners) to generate financial returns. The way they do it is by allocating capital to risky assets - startups.

One of the most critical responsibilities of the VC is effective portfolio construction, or deciding on a set of companies it wants to invest in to achieve the best returns. Although textbooks say that "every company a VC bets on must have a chance to return the whole fund", the reality is much more complex. It may sometimes make sense for the venture firm to invest in companies that have the potential to increase the value of the existing investments even if the new portfolio company itself is unlikely to become a homerun. For instance, although service players typically result in lower return multiples than product startups, having a security services provider distribute products of other portfolio companies can help them grow much faster. Moreover, since most VCs raise a new fund every 3-5 years, having companies in their portfolio that can exit quickly and earn relatively modest returns can be as good as having investments that will appreciate greatly on paper but won't see an exit for a decade.

The VC landscape is diverse and complex:

- Different VC firms have different areas of focus or thesis. The thesis is established when VCs raise capital from their own investors, and it doesn't typically change. A firm with a mission to invest in immigrant founders won't make an "exception" for a startup that doesn't meet this criteria. The thesis can be fairly broad: for example, a VC that has a mandate to invest in space technology can most certainly write a check to a cybersecurity startup securing space tech infrastructure.
- Different VCs specialize in companies at different stages. For example, a firm may only invest in Series A and B, which means that a seed-stage startup is very unlikely to get funding from this VC until it reaches the right milestone. Exceptions are possible (such as a small check to secure an allocation in the next round) but not commonplace.
- Different VC firms have different approaches to investing, portfolio construction, growth strategies, hiring, running boards, and other matters. Most of this isn't written on their websites and the only way to learn about it is by talking to other founders and asking the right questions in conversations with the firms' partners. Some, for example, will only invest in companies with two or more technical co-founders, while others have a go-to-market playbook which they expect their portfolio companies will execute after the round closes. Understanding how different VC firms operate can help founders make the best decisions for their business.

These are just some of the nuances; there is much more. The VC space is undeniably complex and often hard to navigate, but founders should not focus on the nuances more than they need to. The reality is that great companies will rarely have any issues getting funding on good terms, while those that offer little promise, will struggle regardless of how much they know about venture capital. Entrepreneurs should focus on their customers and their business; the rest will fall into place as they progress on their journey.

Expert Insight

"Founders need to know their audience before stepping into a first meeting with a VC. During the first meeting, the investor is evaluating a startup on five dimensions — market, team, product, metrics, and valuation/deal dynamics. Early-stage investors are laser-focused on the market and the founding team given the other three points are either non-existent or less relevant. They are thinking about what is happening more broadly in the sector, how this could create a new entry point, and why this founding team will have an edge in building a multi-billion-dollar startup in this fledgling category. Late-stage investors also assess the market and team but have the advantage of diving into the product and understanding competitive differentiation as well as the ability to assess SaaS metrics and evaluate multi-year sales pipeline. Early-stage investors focus on helping founders go from zero to one and find early product-market fit while late-stage investors help founders scale globally and provide advice on how to build a platform company. The right VC at the right stage can have a material positive impact on the founder's journey."

- Sid Trivedi, Partner at Foundation Capital

Corporate venture capital funds

Corporate venture capital: fundamentals

Corporate venture capital, commonly abbreviated as CVC, is a way by which large, established companies invest in startups. The two main motivators for such investments are strategic and financial considerations. Firms that have a strategic mandate, are looking for alignment between the offerings of the CVC's parent and the focus of the portfolio company. For example, the parent enterprise might be looking to get a stake in a core capability it is reliant on, or build stronger ties with a company it wants to integrate or launch a joint venture with. Financially-motivated corporate venture funds have a sole mission of leveraging the available capital to generate the highest possible investment returns. Unlike strategics, financially-driven CVCs often operate fully independently from their parent company which is treated solely as a supplier of capital. Most corporate venture funds fall somewhere in between the two extremes. For example, a CVC may have a mandate to look for potential alignment with the parent but do it in a way that is not going to lead to investments with poor projected returns.

There was a time when corporate venture capital firms needed an impressive office on Sand Hill Road, a large team with a Chief Financial Officer (CFO), legal counsel, and executive admin. Today's CVCs are lean: 1-2 partners who make investments and build bridges with the corporate side, an associate, and an ability to leverage roughly 3-10% of the time of people already handling finance, legal, technical strategy, and other critical functions of the CVC's parent firm. The fund sizes are smaller, and most of the funds are evergreen which means they are able to receive capital as needed, and not limited to the fund size initially announced. It can be said that doing corporate ventures has been demystified with simple, straightforward models that can be adopted by enterprises with little to no modifications.

Every CVC has its operating practices: some write large checks and take board seats while most co-invest relatively modest amounts alongside the lead VC and become board observers. Most corporate venture funds want the startup to have at least one or two enterprise customers to see a path where they can work together. The terms have become very founder-friendly (it's extremely rare to see anyone requesting a right of first refusal, as an example). CVCs run by cybersecurity companies (there are a few of them now), tend to act similarly to cyber-focused VC funds while corporate ventures at firms outside of security are more akin to generalist VCs.

Strategic CVCs and their motivations

While the motivation of financially driven CVCs is self-explanatory, strategic corporate investors deserve additional discussion.

To continue growing, established enterprises need to ensure the existence of strong ecosystems - standards, organizations, businesses, and technologies that support or amplify the value of their offerings. One of the ways to do it is by investing in startups aligned with the mission of the business. Ecosystems powered by API connectivity and marketplace opportunities are arguably some of the most important drivers of corporate venture capital investments today.

Market development is the second common motivator that leads the strategic CVC's investment decisions. This includes investments in companies with the potential to act as resellers and distributors of the core technology (say, security service providers), as well as those that can influence distribution and shape demand trends in emerging market segments.

Enterprises recognize that they cannot solve all problems themselves, hence why technologies which fill gaps in their portfolio are another common type of company strategic CVCs are often paying attention to. This is especially the case in cybersecurity where deep domain expertise is required to tackle small yet impactful use cases. Security demands the ability to integrate a multitude of tools, and most cybersecurity firms have an app store or integration directory. Security companies can avoid building all the capabilities themselves by choosing the right partners and providing them with capital and support to grow.

Value proposition of corporate venture funds

As capital has become a commodity, it is how corporate ventures differentiate that matters. The main way CVCs stand out in the crowded market is by designing different ways to add value post-investment.

The strongest value proposition of CVCs are established customer base and distribution channels with the ability for two-way referrals, global brand recognition, and technical know-how. The value-add that can be offered by corporate venture funds include:

- Enhanced exposure within the marketplace and the ecosystem of companies and technologies that are deeply embedded into the enterprise's core product offering. Being featured on the integrations marketplace of a large vendor can be a powerful boost for the startup generating brand awareness and demand for their product. This alone will most likely not make or break the business - while useful, it will by no means replace the startup's need to look for independent ways to grow.
- A potential to broaden the reach and increase adoption by building co-marketing partnerships with the enterprise. Startups that receive investment from a CVC, can often get the CVC's parent company to become a paying customer. While the deployment size may not be large, the marketing materials produced from such collaboration, such as case studies and video testimonials, are invaluable.
- Access to insights, guidance, and knowledge base from the network of mentors with experience in sales and go-to-market strategy, positioning, product, engineering, and finance, to name a few. Some CVCs provide startups with resources such as recruiting, marketing, and technology advice, while others organize webinars, workshops, and "ask me anything" sessions that cover anything from finance and operations to roadmap planning.

- Aside from potentially helping with the go-to-market and customer introductions, corporate venture funds can connect startups to industry analysts, security leaders from their networks, media, and prospective technical or channel partners.
- Exclusive insight into the product roadmap of CVC's parent company. This is not a default value proposition and it is not something all corporate VCs can offer, but it can be incredibly useful if the startup heavily relies on the enterprise product developed by the CVC's parent.

Effective ways to work with corporate venture funds

In a large company, things do not simply "happen" by having the CVC pass the deal to the partnerships team, hence not every corporate venture can deliver on its promises. To move initiatives forward and navigate the inherent complexity of large enterprises, the CVC needs to have the right relationships with the right people. Founders evaluating a corporate venture fund should understand if it has effective ways to involve leaders from different parts of the enterprise in its work. For instance, if executives from across the organization are a part of due diligence, or shaping the strategic direction of the CVC, it is much more likely they will be bought in and interested in supporting the portfolio companies post-investment.

Another area founders need to understand is what systems and processes the CVC was able to put in place and what resources it has to move its initiatives forward. For example, signing a two-way referral agreement will not do much unless there is someone capable of designing the right incentive structure so that account executives in the CVC's enterprise know about the startup, have all the necessary sales enablement materials, and most importantly, can get compensated for selling the partner's product. There need to be ways and a willingness to measure success such as tracking how many times the product is mentioned in sales calls and what amount of revenue comes from a referral. Even a simple task of creating a marketing testimonial should have an owner - there is someone who will be on the video, someone who will finance its production, someone in charge of filming and editing, as well as getting the sign-off from the enterprise's PR team.

Most founders tend to be somewhat short-sighted when getting investments from corporate VCs, thinking "We got their logo as a customer and a marketing testimonial, so that's great". This mindset prevents them from getting the value that CVCs could offer in other areas - around technological expertise, industry insights, and a strong network of partners, to name a few. Moreover, many entrepreneurs assume that getting funded by the CVC sets the stage for the potential acquisition. While it could happen, there are so many variables that impact the M&A decision-making that it would be very unreasonable to think that a CVC would invest in a startup solely to accelerate a potential future acquisition. More importantly, the market will look different a few years after funding, and a startup's competitors may be in a better position to get bought. Another company may become a market leader, or the opposite - a competitor might be faltering so it might make more sense to buy it at a low price point. When thinking about getting an investment from a corporate venture firm, founders should optimize for the near term instead of trying to predict the future many years ahead.

Expert Insight

"Founder's expectations of strategic investor's potential to support go-to-market and product development are often too low. Founders should be proactive and ask CVCs they are talking to for real case studies on how they've helped their portfolio companies and conduct both on-list and off-list references to ask the tougher questions founder-to-founder such as: 'Did the corporation introduce you to any customers? Did any of those introductions close and for how much added revenue? How exactly is the company's sales field incentivized to sell your product? How fast was the investor to respond? How many contacts internally did the CVC unit link you to in the company? Did you gain any insights from company discussions that led to improvements in your product? Did the company offer investment terms aligned with the market and were they reasonable in their diligence process?'

Only when these questions have qualified answers will you know that you've chosen the right strategic investor to support your business".

- Austin Arensberg, Head of Okta Ventures

Expert Insight

"If you had a corporate job before, imagine getting an email from corporate development from someone you never met, asking for a significant time commitment to help a company they invested in. Most people maybe would do the favor and get on the call, but wouldn't kick off a 2-month long project. At the end of the day, corporate investors don't have authority in the business. What you get out of an investment is a friend in the company. They can get people to take a call, but it's your responsibility to convince them to partner."

- Lior Yaari, Co-Founder and CEO at Grip Security

Deep Dive

To get the list of CVCs that invest in cybersecurity, check out a Venture in Security deep dive titled "Corporate venture capital and cybersecurity: why Okta, CrowdStrike, CyberArk and others invest in cybersecurity startups". You can find it by navigating to https://ventureinsecurity.net/p/corporate-venture-capital-and-cybersecurity or by scanning this QR code.

Influencers

There is a category of rarely discussed players in the cybersecurity space that wields a lot of power in the industry. I call them "influencers" as they shape demand, influence the behaviors of buyers, and even create new markets. The three parties with the outsized impact on cybersecurity are industry analysts, insurance companies, and government regulators.

The way the demand for security products and services is created is complex and highly nuanced. The behavior of adversaries and the emergence of new technologies establishes what are known as "attack vectors" - ways in which attackers enter a network, application, or a system. Security entrepreneurs recognize the need to address the gap in the market and start companies that reduce either the probability, or the impact of security incidents, or in some cases both.

Although startup founders do their very best to promote their approaches and solutions, buyers don't automatically rush to purchase and deploy new tools. It takes time for the need to be understood; industry analysts, insurance companies, and government regulators play a critical role in establishing and solidifying this understanding.

By talking to cybersecurity startup founders and enterprise security teams, industry analysts learn about the problems on the market, and the wide variety of solutions designed to address them. By applying rigorous research methodologies, looking for patterns, and aggregating insights, analysts declare the creation of new market categories. Additionally, industry analysts further evangelize the need for certain categories and shortlist the solutions they think CISOs should consider. Analyst activity greatly influences the buyers' behavior in the enterprise market.

The primary role of the government is to protect the public interest, ensuring order, safety and security is a critical part of this. When security incidents happen, businesses and ordinary citizens lose sensitive data, money, and sometimes even lives. To prevent cybersecurity breaches which have the potential of severe consequences from becoming commonplace, the government issues regulations. The government's intervention creates demand for security products and services, and since the providers of these products and services know it, they actively lobby for more compliance and regulatory oversight.

Unlike the government, which relies on political will to achieve its objectives, the insurance industry is a market force with the power to influence the dynamics and demand for products and services in the cybersecurity space. By focusing on their own business goals, insurance companies design requirements, systems, and incentives that seek to reduce underwriting loss ratios and increase profitability. One of the by-products of this process is the maturation of the security industry.

Industry analysts

Industry analyst firms: fundamentals

Industry analyst firms are organizations that employ analysts whose role is to know the industry, its products, people, and trends. Industry analysts are not like your traditional cybersecurity analyst: rather than having significant technical domain expertise, they are usually (but not always) individuals with years of broader experience in enterprise environments who have a mixture of knowledge covering technology, business, and more.

Analysts add value to the cybersecurity ecosystem by:

- Publishing research about market trends, technologies, and forces shaping the future of the industry.
- Conducting vendor briefings - talking to different companies on the market, learning about their products and services, and distilling their learnings into easy-to-understand summaries.
- Answering vendors' questions about the market, product, and the go-to-market strategy.

- Advising enterprise business and security leaders about vendors, products, and the most effective ways to tackle problems they are facing.
- Organizing events and webinars, speaking at industry conferences, and engaging in other forms of thought leadership.

Industry analyst firms play a unique role in the market by simultaneously selling subscriptions to their services to two groups of customers: security vendors and buyers. That said, most advisory firms sell primarily, and some - exclusively to security vendors.

Security vendors buy subscriptions as a way to access the research, which often includes useful insights into buyer behavior, but most importantly enables them to spend more time with the analysts. The more time they spend with analysts, the stronger the relationship and the more likely analysts will keep their solutions top of mind when customers come to ask for recommendations, or when analysts make public comments about representative solutions to a particular problem.

Security organizations buy subscriptions to get access to the research, but most importantly, also to spend time with the analysts. They come with questions such as "What tool is the best in the market for X or Y" and "How should I tackle problem Z in my organization?". Oftentimes, they don't know what questions to ask, in which case it becomes a part of the analyst's job to guide them in the right direction. Many analysts have hundreds if not thousands of these conversations every year, which helps them discern trends, common questions, and more.

Expert Insight

"Cybersecurity and the many topics included and orthogonal to it, enable the business to achieve more; it is not solely deployed for restricting user actions. Security is now foundational to business growth to support collaboration and data sharing, supply chain management, end user engagement, and successful ecommerce. However, vendors and buy-side acquirers often find it difficult to link technical capabilities with the key business objectives.

What to measure? How to select? What does success look like? The analyst's role today is often more about helping the vendor uncover their narrative in the context of business problems whilst simultaneously helping the acquirer mine the complex world of acronyms and technical marketing soup to map requirements to capabilities."

- Simon Moffatt, Founder and Research Analyst at The Cyber Hut

Industry analysts wield a lot of influence

Industry analysts greatly influence the purchasing process of large enterprises. There are several reasons why that is the case.

Cybersecurity is a complicated and broad field that requires many different technologies and knowledge areas. Most people are good at a few: for example, a CISO with a background in network security would benefit from advice about hardening defenses for the cloud, and a team strong on prevention would need help learning about detection & response. Security leaders' full-time job is to safeguard their organizations, not to follow every emerging market or know every single technology that's available, especially across the entirety of cybersecurity.

Making decisions in this chaotic space with new threats (and new products to fight them) created daily is nearly impossible, especially at large organizations with complex environments and thousands of factors to consider. Security executives in Fortune 1000 companies are looking for external parties to help make sense of all the cacophony of signals. Industry analyst firms play this role of such parties.

Analysts are full-time market experts, with a top-down, rather than a bottom-up view. With enough end-user feedback, they act as a safe and anonymous conduit for sharing peer information. They gather and redistribute insights about what different organizations in similar circumstances are doing, how security teams across various companies compare against one another, and what approaches have (or haven't) worked for them. By providing a shortlist of vendors, easy-to-navigate charts, rigorous research, and professional advice, analysts not only de-risk decision-making for individual security leaders, but also help secure approvals and buy-in from other departments involved in the purchasing process, such as legal, finance, operations, procurement, and compliance.

Another reason why industry analysts are so important is the fact that in security, the quality of what is being bought and sold is not easily known. If a company is purchasing, say, an accounting tool, it can evaluate if the product does what it claims to do. The same is true for most if not all, other types of software but not for cybersecurity. A team buying a security product cannot easily validate and be certain that in critical moments, the product will perform as what was promised.

Biases at analyst firms

Many people assume that industry analysts are biased and "pay to play", which refers to the practice of altering research results - vendor rankings, opinions, and reports - influenced by commercial relationships. The reality is much more complex.

All the analysts I know are objective and unbiased people who are deeply knowledgeable and passionate about the future of security. More so, despite the never-ending rumors of the "pay to play", I have not come across any documented evidence of that happening in the top-tier firms. Large companies have strict rules about conflict of interest and would terminate any analyst who does not disclose such a conflict. The same, however, cannot always be said about a select few small firms that write "whitepapers" and "research" paid for and approved by vendors that are then used for lead generation.

Two factors lead to the perceived subjectivity of industry analyst firms:

1. Industry analysts operate in a system that by design, creates a huge potential for conflict of interest. Analyst firms take money from two sides with diametrically opposite interests:

sellers who pay with the intent to generate demand for their products, and buyers paying for objective advice

2. Industry analysts have limited information about the vendors they evaluate. When analysts write reviews of security tools, they normally do it based on product demos and discussions with company customers who agree to provide references for the vendor; in the case of emerging vendors and markets, the ratio of vendors to customers might be as high as 5:1. The perspective analysts develop without being hands-on, and testing the tool in an appropriate environment, can be of limited value to customers and industry insiders. Even if analysts were formerly hands-on technical professionals, this knowledge ages out quickly

The other incorrect assumption is that security companies can pay analyst firms to get great reviews. Vendor briefings with analysts - calls where startups explain what they do - are free and accessible to any startup, usually just gated by an analyst's research interests. What vendors are actually paying for is the ability to spend more time with analysts. The subscription enables them to ask questions, show what they do, and importantly - build a relationship with the analyst. This doesn't mean that analysts are going to only say good things about the company; what matters is that they are more likely to remember the vendor when writing reports and talking to enterprises who come for advice.

Working with industry analysts

Given the number of vendors in the space, it's no wonder that companies that invest in analyst relations are much more likely to be recommended as potential solutions to customer problems. For founders targeting startups or consumer segments, industry analysts will be much less useful, but for companies selling to enterprises, engaging with analysts is essential. If you regularly engage with industry analysts, over time they can become great champions whenever you need an independent party to talk to the press, investors, customers, or even potential acquirers.

Engaging with analyst firms is often referred to as "analyst relations" and is a function that usually falls under marketing. For a startup, this may fall to the founder while wearing their "marketing" hat, a dedicated marketing team, or via an external agency providing marketing services. Larger vendors will typically have dedicated individuals or teams for analyst relations.

There are generally three ways cybersecurity founders can engage with industry analysts: by holding vendor briefings, by reaching out for an inquiry, or by contracting firms for content.

Vendor briefings are a free way for founders to talk to the analyst and explain, among other things, what problem they are trying to solve, for whom, and why it matters. Briefings are more one-way (founders or executives briefing the analyst); depending on the analyst firm, analysts will generally not answer questions from the vendor or provide any kind of advice.

Inquiries, on the other hand, are reserved for subscribers (vendors or end user organizations) and are structured to have the analyst answer questions, usually submitted in advance, about their specific areas or research. A vendor firm may use an inquiry to ask the analyst about their opinion of the market, or use the time to pre-test a new public message.

Many analyst firms can also be contracted to provide content to be used in public, usually in support of expanding visibility for the brand. This may be an analyst presentation at a webinar or customer event, a custom piece of research, and others.

Here are some of the tips about engaging industry analysts:

- Make sure you are talking to the right analyst - the one who covers your (or adjacent) market segment.
- Be clear about your vision, your place in the market, and what makes you different.
- Show, not tell: show a product demo instead of long slide decks.
- Provide reference customers - their word will be worth 100x what you say.

- Be open and don't lie or overestimate reality.
- If you are a subscriber to an analyst firm, turn this into a regular (quarterly, biannual) update, not a press-release-like statement.
- Be helpful, be respectful, and focus on building a relationship - it's a long-term game for everyone involved.
- Pay attention to the questions they ask - if analysts don't understand something, it may be a sign that your messaging needs some refinement.
- Note that you might need to schedule calls several weeks or months in advance so be sure to plan ahead.
- Many analysts attend industry events and are open to chatting then. That said, a conversation at an event is not the time for a briefing, but much more for building relationships.
- Playing games like thinking that if you can fool the analyst, they will drive business your way, will backfire. The best way to annoy an analyst is to compromise their credibility.

If you choose to become a paying customer of an analyst firm, many analysts can help with marketing, go-to-market strategy, sales, product, and more. I believe that these services are geared toward large vendors and are of very limited value for most startups. To succeed as a startup, founders must learn by doing, stay in close contact with their customers, and should not look for shortcuts like analysts or market research firms. Having said that, it is useful to understand the broader industry context, what other companies have tried, what has worked for them, and what hasn't. It is worth noting that some analyst firms are open to offering a free inquiry session as a trial - something founders can and most definitely should take advantage of.

Expert Insight

"I think it is important for founders to understand a couple of things.

First, the industry analyst landscape for cybersecurity consists of dozens if not hundreds of firms. The market is heavily skewed toward the big 3 - Gartner, Forrester, and IDC - but several other firms exist and may be able to support founders in different ways.

Second, that analysts have distinct needs from sales prospects. Usually, analysts want to understand a vendor from two perspectives: as a technology provider but also as a business. This means understanding not only the details of a vendor offering but also how that vendor is approaching go-to-market, partnerships, trends, and more."

- Fernando Montenegro, Senior Principal Analyst at Omdia

Insurance companies

Insurance companies: fundamentals

The insurance industry goes hundreds of years back, and its impact on our modern society in general, and the maturation of cybersecurity in particular, is hard to overestimate.

At the core, purchasing insurance is an act of transferring the potential risk of losses to a third party in exchange for an amount of money, called an insurance premium. The business model of insurance is often misunderstood as many people assume that companies in the industry make money by increasing the difference between the premiums they charge and the losses they are willing to cover. That is only partially true. Insurance companies estimate the probability of risk occurrence and the maximum amount of loss if the risk event does occur, price the coverage to reflect the level of risk the firm is taking, collect policy premiums from the policyholders before the risk event happens, invest the capital collected, and when claims happen, cover the losses up to the previously specified maximum.

In insurance, there are two main income streams: underwriting income and interest income. To put it simply, underwriting income is the difference between the premiums collected and the losses paid. To maximize profitability, insurance companies are incentivized to charge as much premiums to as many customers as possible, without losing the guard so much that they overpromise to cover losses to those with unacceptably high chances of loss occurrence. Although insurance firms would like their premiums to be as high as possible, the competition on the market and the fact that buyers see insurance as a commodity keep the prices in check.

To maximize their underwriting income, insurance companies set the minimum qualification requirements for the buyers. This allows them to make sure that policy buyers have at least some basic protection and prevention measures that lower the probability and impact of loss. For example, a firm issuing a cybersecurity policy would require that the policyholders use password managers and multi-factor authentication (MFA). Some insurance companies go further and design incentives that encourage their customers to take measures that reduce risk. For example, they may offer discounts to holders of cybersecurity insurance that have a comprehensive security program, regular employee training, and good patching hygiene.

While this is where most people's understanding of the insurance business model ends, this is where the real story begins. Because insurance collects premiums today, and the potential claims will happen tomorrow, it sits on a large pool of capital called "float". The way insurance makes most of the money is by reinvesting the premiums into other interest-generating assets such as stocks and bonds. The more premiums the insurance firm collects and keeps in its bank accounts, the more interest income it can receive.

In his 2010 letter to Berkshire Hathaway shareholders, Warren Buffet explained the impact of float on the insurance business well: "Insurers receive premiums upfront and pay claims later... This collect-now, pay-later model leaves us holding large sums - money we call "float" - that will eventually go to others. Meanwhile, we get to invest this float for Berkshire's benefit... If premiums exceed the total of expenses and eventual losses, we register an underwriting profit that adds to the investment income produced from the float. This combination allows us to enjoy the use of free money - and, better yet, get paid for holding it. Alas, the hope of this happy result attracts intense competition, so vigorous in most years as to cause the P/C industry as a whole to operate at a significant underwriting loss. This loss, in effect, is what the industry pays to hold its float. Usually this cost is fairly low, but in some catastrophe-ridden years the cost from underwriting losses more than eats up the income derived from use of float...".

Challenges of insuring cybersecurity losses

The probability of cyber risk occurrence, and most importantly, the factors leading to it are not yet well understood. Intuitively, we know that having security training is going to reduce the chances that someone will click on a phishing link, but with attackers becoming better at social engineering, it is getting increasingly harder to assume that tomorrow's threats will look like yesterday's "Nigerian prince" email scam. Many companies that get breached do have written security policies in place, are "compliant" with different regulatory requirements, and have some (often "best-of-breed") security tooling deployed in their environment. With the ever-growing number of attack vectors, it becomes next to impossible to shortlist the factors that matter as they all do. Every account can be compromised. Every email can be used for a phishing attempt. Every piece of hardware and all software contains vulnerabilities that can be discovered and exploited at any time. Modeling anything in these circumstances is not a simple exercise. Moreover, since every organization is unique and requires different approaches to securing it, providing one-size-fits-all product recommendations beyond the basics like password managers and MFA is not always effective.

Because technology is interconnected, a breach at one company can affect hundreds and thousands of other businesses globally; we have had plenty of examples of that happening in the past. When this happens, the magnitude of losses can be insurmountable as the company that failed to protect its networks can fold under the pressure of lawsuits from others who suffered because of it. The same problem of everything being interconnected in invisible ways makes it impossible for cybersecurity insurance providers to decorrelate potential losses. This is the biggest challenge surrounding cyber insurance as it prevents the insurance firm's ability to avoid disaster events. One thousand businesses from all over the country operating in different industries are very unlikely to catch fire or get flooded all on the same day. However, it is entirely possible that most or even all of them would suffer from the same ransomware attack encrypting data and rendering their computer networks unusable. The fact that it is not currently possible to decorrelate cyber risk, leads some people in the industry to argue that cybersecurity risk is systemic, and as such it should not be insurable.

Expert Insight

"One of the biggest challenges insurance companies face when entering the cyber world is the cost of evaluating a claim. While in traditional insurance claims, the cost of the adjustor is minimal, in the cyber world, once a party has claimed a breach, the cost the insurance company incurs just to verify if a breach had really happened can be in the tens of thousands. It's a new era for insurance companies and it will take both the insurance world and the cyber world some time to adjust."

- Yochai Greenberg, Co-Founder and CTO at Nano Cyber Solutions

Impact of insurance on the cybersecurity industry

Cyber insurance has been a major influencer of the demand for security products and solutions worldwide, accelerating the maturation of security practices. Unlike the government, which typically requires years of discussions, consultations, and public hearings to make a decision based on citizen involvement and broad societal consensus, the insurance industry is much more flexible and is able to move fast. Moreover, while regulators can only enforce laws within the boundaries of their states and countries, insurance standards are global since the business and the economy are global as well.

Over the past decade, insurance providers have continuously raised the minimum requirements surrounding the eligibility for cyber coverage, therefore forcing the maturation of security practices across different industries and geographies. Their role in pushing the industry forward continues to grow: since insurance companies see the details and intricacies of thousands of cyber breaches that don't become a matter of public knowledge, they are best positioned to spot trends and recommend solutions to reduce the frequency and severity of security incidents.

Other ways in which insurance can accelerate the maturation of security practices are establishing and adopting industry standards, educating individuals and businesses about the importance of cybersecurity, and facilitating cross-border, cross-industry knowledge sharing.

Cyber insurance for founders

Founders of security products and services must remember that cyber insurance is a major influencer in the technology market. There are many ways to use this understanding to help advance the industry.

First, by helping insurance companies understand how a certain measure or approach reduces risk, startups can increase the chances that security best practices will become a requirement for obtaining coverage or a way to reduce policy premiums. This, in turn, can drive demand for products and services that benefit policyholders and help them manage risk.

Second, although most insurance companies do not directly sell or recommend specific solutions, many have explicit criteria for tooling they would like to see in their customer environments. For example, I have previously come across Excel spreadsheets that detail the features and capabilities of an ideal endpoint security solution. By taking the perspective of insurance providers into account when building products, startup founders can increase the chances that their offerings will be adopted by the broader customer base. Some insurance firms could even be open to providing their policyholders with a list of preferred vendors, be it products or services, offering an opportunity for entrepreneurs to claim them as distribution channels.

Last but not least, the cyber insurance ecosystem includes managed security service providers, as well as digital forensics and incident responders, called to respond to incidents when they happen. Having security service providers work with insurance companies can be a win-win: an insurance firm gets a trusted party ready to respond to a security event, a customer gets the work done quickly and efficiently, and the startup gets a new customer acquisition channel.

Government

Role of the government in cybersecurity

One of the ways in which cybersecurity appears to be a unique field is its relationship with the government. With respect to security, the government is a recruiter, a monopolist, a customer, a talent supplier, a supporter of innovation, and a regulator at the same time.

As a recruiter, the government continuously looks for ways to attract top security professionals. As a supplier of talent, it trains thousands of security practitioners via college and university programs and provides them with practical experience in the field. Career mobility between the public and private sectors is impressive: it is hard to find another industry where the government experience would offer a great stepping stone for a leadership role in the private sector. In cybersecurity, these transitions are routine, and alumni of the military, law enforcement, and intelligence agencies are often highly sought after by businesses looking for experienced security leaders.

The government holds the monopoly on force, which allows it to fulfill its duty as a defender and guardian of law and order. Working for the government and the various branches of intelligence agencies is seen as one of the few dream places for technical red teamers. As a part of the defense budget, the government pumps significant capital into research and development (R&D) as well as offensive and defensive cyber warfare capabilities.

Given the number of unique risks faced by businesses in different sectors, geographies, sizes, and industry verticals, the government cannot hope to provide actionable and relevant recommendations for every company. What it does have the ability to do is to facilitate the collaboration between different organizations, and enable knowledge sharing among them. This can be highly impactful as the behaviors of industry leaders tend to be mirrored by others across the market, making it possible to disseminate best practices organically, through knowledge sharing and collaboration. Examples of successful models when it comes to cyber threat information sharing are Information Sharing and Analysis Centers (ISACs), Information Sharing and Analysis Organizations (ISAOs), and Cybersecurity and Infrastructure Security Agency (CISA). The government has shown that it is capable of sharing cybersecurity threat intelligence with security teams and service providers, making it easier to understand the threat landscape and get the upper hand against attackers.

Other ways through which the government gets to impact the state of cyber defense include:

- Encouraging investment in cyber defense through various forms of public-private partnerships and unique arrangements such as the taxpayer-funded venture capital firm In-Q-Tel, a venture arm of the Central Intelligence Agency (CIA).
- Funding cybersecurity-focused research, such as that directed at securing critical infrastructure (think of the work of DARPA in the US).
- In collaboration with the private sector, establishing apprenticeship programs to help train the next generation of cybersecurity professionals.
- Gaining access to networks and systems where adversaries operate, tracking their activities, and stepping in when required if there is a threat to the critical infrastructure or national security.

Government as a customer and a regulator

The two roles of the government that are of particular interest to cybersecurity entrepreneurs are that of a customer and a regulator.

In any country, the government, its various agencies, and organizations under its oversight are the largest buyers of cybersecurity solutions. The government's scale of deployment, length of contracts, retention, and willingness to pay make it a perfect customer for any security company capable of delivering products and services at a nearly infinite scale. Although there are enormous barriers that prevent startups from being able to serve public sector organizations, including bureaucracy and inherent complexity of the public procurement operations, the amount of time and effort required to go through the sales process, and the overall resistance to changes and new technologies, being able to secure government contracts is widely seen as a sign of great maturity. Large security, cloud, and infrastructure providers are actively working to expand their already deep relationships with the government, often by hiring ex-public sector employees with deep connections in the field to lead their government relations (GR) and sales functions.

As a regulator, the government has the ability to set and enforce standards and define what constitutes an acceptable level of security. The process of setting security regulations has two forces pushing and pulling in different directions. On one side, there are cybersecurity vendors and advocacy groups who want to see new security standards and stricter regulations. Security-focused groups see them as a necessity to ensure that the nation can protect itself from adversaries, while vendors welcome regulations because they drive demand for their products and services, and even create new markets. On the other hand, large enterprises such as Fortune 500 organizations would prefer to avoid regulatory scrutiny and have fewer compliance requirements to worry about. Both parties employ government relations professionals, commonly known as lobbyists, that help them fight for their cause.

Lobbying cybersecurity regulations

When people think about lobbying, what they often picture is a complex net of perverse incentives, covert motivations, and hidden figures trying to sway government leaders to take their positions. The reality of lobbying is much more nuanced.

In my view, lobbying for cybersecurity regulation leads to positive outcomes for society as a whole. In other areas of business, I am a big believer in the power of the market to self-regulate; in cybersecurity, I am not as optimistic. Because the private sector focuses on maximizing shareholder value and increasing profits, without appropriate regulation and mechanisms for enforcement it will typically look to implement the minimum measures which allow it to achieve these goals. There is a shared understanding among security leaders, practitioners, and policymakers that we need to do better when it comes to cybersecurity. Businesses of all sizes need to make sure they implement measures that can protect them from cyberattacks and safeguard customer data.

To ensure that those with the ability to shape the state of the industry get the necessary information to make decisions that promote cyber-secure behaviors and help safeguard people's data, cybersecurity entrepreneurs need to be intentional about their efforts.

Lobbying is first and foremost the process of educating decision-makers about the importance of security. Large tech companies have people whose role is to be fully focused on government relations; startups without sufficient resources have to become creative. The following are some of the ways in which cybersecurity entrepreneurs can help educate the industry about the importance of security:

- Joining and collaborating with industry groups - vendor alliances, associations, networks, and councils such as ISACs.
- Working with government agencies, serving on not-for-profit boards and advisory councils, and participating in citizen committees.
- Sharing thought leadership in media, publishing books, and collaborating with academic institutions on research.

- Organizing press conferences, expert panels, demonstrations, and other events.

Lobbying is about sharing perspectives and ideas that advance the cause and make it easy for decision-makers to understand why they should care. By educating the public, security entrepreneurs can wield a lot of power in the space and help move the industry forward.

Expert Insight

"As software becomes increasingly pervasive to every aspect of society from consumer goods to critical infrastructure and national security, governments will increasingly play a role in the software ecosystem and cybersecurity. This includes as a buyer, often serving as the single largest consumer of technology and software in their nations, such as in the U.S., leading to long-term financially large contracts and procurements. This also includes as a regulatory and governance body, striving to ensure insecure software and products don't present unacceptable risks to consumers, customers, national interests and security. Any cybersecurity builder looking to scale their product(s) and organizations must be familiar with the role of government, the complex procurement process and pathways as well as applicable and evolving regulatory and legal considerations that can impact a cybersecurity company's strategic objectives."

- Chris Hughes, Co-Founder and President at Aquia, Cyber Innovation Fellow at Cybersecurity and Infrastructure Security Agency (CISA)

Distributors

Importance of channel partners in cybersecurity sales

To build a successful cybersecurity company, it is not enough to ship great products: a startup must set up a scalable distribution model. Finding a way to get the solution in the hands of customers is anything but easy.

When most people think about distribution in cybersecurity, what comes to mind are aggressive sales representatives calling the personal phone numbers of CISOs and sending hundreds of unsolicited emails to the inboxes of security practitioners. While all that is indeed happening, it may surprise many readers to learn that according to the research firm Canalys (https://canalys.com/), $9 out of $10 in security is spent via the so-called channel partners - resellers, integrators, consultancies, and security service providers, to name a few. The world's largest enterprises don't have the infrastructure to buy directly from vendors. Instead, they rely on exclusive agreements with select value-added resellers and other partners to recommend the right solutions, set the price, and ultimately close deals.

Channel partners sell products from established vendors to large enterprises. To reach smaller enterprises or mid-market customers, security companies can go direct, leveraging their own sales teams. Startups have no choice at all since channel partners don't resell solutions from small, up-and-coming providers. That is why they hire armies of salespeople to call every security leader they can reach, and hopefully get them to agree to attend a demo.

Needless to say, the way cybersecurity products are bought and sold is archaic, especially when compared to modern areas of technology such as developer tooling or data infrastructure. Many founders quickly get disillusioned about what it takes to get their tool in customers' hands and close a contract. It is not uncommon to see visionary practitioners reject these traditional go-to-market approaches altogether, hoping that new ideas alone such as product-led growth can propel them to grow and achieve market leadership.

I believe smart cybersecurity entrepreneurs need to take a pragmatic approach to sales. This means first and foremost being realistic about the state of the market and acknowledging the gap between where many would like the security industry to be, and where it currently is. Embracing the reality is not about limiting one's options and doing things the way they have always been done, but doing what brings the right results today while recognizing that tomorrow will look different. It's critical to continue experimenting with new approaches and testing other ways to acquire customers.

In this chapter, I cover the current state of the channel partner ecosystem. Later in the book, I am going to discuss different go-to-market strategies more broadly and zoom in on the opportunities brought by emerging distribution channels including selling through vCISOs and via large platforms of security vendors and cloud providers. Before we think big and imagine what could be possible, it's important to ground ourselves in the present and understand where we are and how things are done today.

Role of the channel partners in the tech ecosystem

A startup's growth potential is often constrained by its access to capital, the ability to attract the right talent, and the systems and processes it puts in place. Getting from $0 to $1M ARR can be done solely because the founders are true hustlers; growing from $1M to $10M can be achieved by expanding the company's sales force. Going to $100M and above in annual recurring revenue while only relying on internal resources is hard, often not possible, and generally unnecessary because of the presence of important market players - channel partners.

Although as I mentioned, over $9 out of every $10 enterprise security is spent via the channel, channel partnerships are not a cybersecurity invention: they are a critical part of the distribution network for all kinds of products and services. Take Shopify, one of the world's largest e-commerce platforms, as an example: in 2019, the company's revenue was around $1.5B whereas the partner ecosystem generated more than $6.9B. The 2021 State of the Channel Report found that the leading cloud providers - Microsoft, Google, and Amazon are moving away from direct sales and doubling down on channel partnerships. Microsoft, for instance, has been heavily relying on its partner ecosystem to deliver products and services to end customers; as of 2019, the partner ecosystem was responsible for 95% of Microsoft's commercial revenue.

Types of channel partners in cybersecurity

Channel partners are critical for cybersecurity because no company can reach millions of businesses around the world on its own. Establishing and maintaining relationships spanning countries, languages, time zones, and industries is not feasible without reliance on partner networks.

The term "channel partner" is quite vague as it does not delineate the variety of players and business models that exist around the general bucket of "cybersecurity service providers". In the context of security, the following are the typical players in the channel space:

- Strategy consultancies that help companies establish & manage their security strategy.
- Resellers/value-added resellers (VARs) that help companies select vendors so that the security strategy can be implemented.
- Integrators that decompose the strategy into separate projects, bring experienced engineers and architects to handle technical implementation of security solutions and tailor technical capabilities to solve customer problems.
- Managed security service providers (MSSPs) and managed detection & response services (MDRs) that take care of the ongoing security management, custom detection work, monitoring, and support.
- Managed service providers (MSPs) that focus primarily on the organizations' IT needs.

Channel partners work with established companies while early-stage startups have to find ways to grow on their own and try hard to get to the point where channel can be interested in distributing what they offer.

Security strategy consultancies

"Cybersecurity consulting" captures a very broad area of services, and when used liberally, it can mean just anything - from strategy to hands-on penetration testing. What is described here focuses on the first step in securing the organization, namely understanding the company's needs and developing a security strategy. While this work is commonly done by security leaders, many companies choose to involve third parties, experienced in developing and implementing effective security strategies across many organizations.

Cybersecurity is one of the fastest-growing types of services offered by the world's largest consulting firms. Companies such as Deloitte, EY, PwC, and KPMG help governments and the private sector understand where they are today in terms of security and how to get to where they want to be tomorrow. First and foremost, they add value by acting as trusted advisors to CISOs and company leadership to understand the business objectives, and the risks the company is facing, as well as its strategic focus to develop a roadmap for implementing holistic security.

Value-add resellers

After the security strategy is completed, the organization needs to select products and tools to have it implemented; this is where resellers come in. The goal of a VAR is to help the customer make sense of the security problems it is facing and bring in the right vendors that integrate and work well with one another. Additionally, VARs help navigate the buying process both from a technical aspect (the value-add) and also a deal negotiation aspect. Because resellers have established relationships with security vendors, and also because they bring a high sales volume, they possess much stronger leverage to get the best pricing arrangement than any individual customer.

Whether or not the customer has been engaging with a consultancy will impact the scope of services a VAR is expected to provide. If there is already a security strategy in place, the reseller would often be working with both the consulting firm and the customer to support them from the product selection standpoint. If, however, the customer came to the reseller directly, the role it would play (and the scope of VAR's value-add) might be much broader. Sometimes, a CISO would come to the VAR saying "I have a network security problem. What should I be looking at and how should I be thinking about the technology to help solve this problem?". The reseller would be able to say "Let's refine our understanding of the problem, look at available options, and make the decision together".

System integrators

Traditionally, in a large firm, there is a need for someone to specialize in the network, endpoint, data and cloud security, data and analytics management, orchestration, automation, and DevOps, as well as application security, to name a few. For an average cybersecurity organization, the task of assembling a diverse team of technical security professionals to configure and later work with technologies needed to secure all facets of the complex environment is not trivial. The initial architecture and integration, in particular, can be incredibly complex.

Whether the company is trying to develop a cloud security program, re-engineer the technology that powers its SOC, and have it work together, system integrators are well equipped to take this challenge on. They are the most hands-on and technical out of all the types of channel partners we've covered so far. Integrators roll up their sleeves and get the hard work done: systems engineering, technical architecture, fine-tuning, extending, and customizing solutions to implement the security strategy, and designing unique integration patterns to make technology do what it needs to do.

While some integrators come in when the technology has been selected, a good systems integrator is typically a part of the technology selection process. Today, however, we see a growing number of cases, when the customer would have already acquired technology or established methods through which it wants to acquire it, long before engaging with the system integrator.

System integrators don't just connect security tools but integrate different pieces into a pattern that works for this particular customer and its specific set of problems. Every client, every vertical, and every domain has different needs, so while different firms might be using the same technology stack, what constitutes an effective integration pattern between these tools is often different. Aside from the technical, hands-on work, system integrators also focus on education. Integrators help customers understand how they can secure their organization, learn how to establish an ongoing process of security assessments, and how to ensure that their security frameworks are aligned with the ever-evolving IT infrastructure and operations.

Managed security service providers (MSSPs)

Once the system integration is complete, a customer has two choices: to do the ongoing security work in-house or to outsource it to a third-party provider. For those who do not find it feasible to hire a leader of the security operations center (SOC) who would build a team of security analysts and security engineers, managed security service providers (MSSPs) can be a viable alternative.

MSSPs are selling security as the outcome of their work. The MSSP's role is to understand the business needs, become an expert on the company's operations and environment, implement protective measures and logic to detect malicious behavior, and continuously monitor the customer's security posture, working through escalations and addressing new risks as they are identified.

A good MSSP provides the ability for customers to entirely outsource the tasks critical for security. In practice, however, instead of outsourcing all of IT, infrastructure management, and security as a whole, most companies today are looking for ways to co-source and/or outsource select parts of IT and security responsibilities that they do not see as feasible or do not have the talent to manage in-house.

Managed service providers (MSPs)

While technically, managed service providers (MSPs) are focused on providing services around the management of IT infrastructure and do not offer security, they deserve an honorary mention here as we see a large number of MSPs trying to move into the MSSP space. This happens as a result of two realizations:

- The realization that MSPs cannot manage the IT stack for customers without having security at the core of how it is done.
- The realization that as IT has become commoditized, and a lot of infrastructure has moved to the cloud, for managed security providers to grow or even to simply preserve their margins, they must expand beyond IT.

Managed security providers see that cybersecurity is becoming table stakes. Today, if two MSPs are competing for the customer, and one offers cybersecurity as a part of the package, while another treats security as a second-class citizen and outsources it to a third party, everything else being equal, the first one will win. It's worth noting that MSPs who are not building and maintaining IT in the cloud with security at the core of how they are thinking about it, won't be viable in the next decade, suffering from cyber breaches and losing customer trust.

Managed service providers interested in expanding their offerings and bundling security are faced with the problem of attracting the right talent. Acquisitions become one of the most viable ways to enter the new market: if an MSP can't hire the right talent, it can buy a strong boutique cybersecurity firm or even a mid-market MSSP player that has already assembled a winning team.

Expert Insight

"It is never immediately obvious at the beginning which specific channel partners will be the best fit for you. The channel will require you to rethink your current marketing initiatives. I have found it best to put yourself into their shoes to help identify what would make your offering most attractive to them.

I would suggest that you very carefully curate your channel partners; instead of a raw number of resellers, it is more important to curate those that have adjacent experience in reselling similar offerings. For example, if the bulk of their sales is in hardware, they might have difficulty in selling security services - they likely do not have the same 'muscle memory' immediately available. It is discouraging to sign up channel partners to only discover several quarters afterward that their salespeople have no interest in selling your offering (indeed, they might not have even known about it!). You must establish within the contract that their salespeople receive quota relief from the sales of your offering.

To make your offering easiest to resell, create extremely specialized and targeted materials that quickly emphasize the benefits they can present to their clients (in the most low-friction manner possible). Ideally, this will require that you bundle and SKU your offerings in the most easy-to-understand manner. Selling your offering to resellers differs from a marketing approach, and you will likely need separate personnel with experience managing the channel early in your journey. If your offering takes considerable time to close a deal, it is critical that you have materials to educate their staff early in any given quarter because if you wait until the end-of-quarter they will revert to what they know how to sell.

Possible problems that may occur with channel partners include early channel contention (e.g. where two different partners compete for the same business deal), and later contention where they find the profit that they have made by reselling your offering is attractive but they could make more money if they sourced it themselves, and as a result substitute a similar (though likely inferior) offering.

The partnership relationship is like most others; it requires ongoing regular care and pruning. If you only tend to your partners once a year (at contract time) you will find yourself bereft of benefits."

- Eldon Sprickerhoff, Founder of eSentire

Acquirers

Paths to an exit for cybersecurity startups

I am a big believer that founders should be looking for ways to grow their companies by solving impactful problems for customers willing to pay to have them solved. Although early-stage founders should be forging ahead instead of daydreaming about how they will exit their companies, it is prudent to understand both what is possible, and what is realistic.

There are three ways cybersecurity entrepreneurs can exit their startups:

- Initial public offering, or an IPO for short.
- A merger with another company.
- An acquisition by a larger player in or outside the industry.

Initial public offering isn't exactly an "exit" so this is certainly an oversimplification. An IPO is just another financing that unlocks the public markets, where new shares get created and sold. Also, companies could go public via Direct Listing, or even the SPAC route. There's also private equity majority recaps instead of a 100% sale which helps existing shareholders take some chips off the table while playing for a bigger outcome. However, these nuances are beyond what an early-stage founder needs to worry about, so for the purposes of our discussion, I'll treat IPOs as a path to an exit the way it is commonly seen.

Of the three, the most probable outcome is the acquisition. Mergers are exceedingly rare and almost don't happen among startups. IPOs are equally unusual: although there are thousands of cybersecurity companies in the US, according to my observations, less than thirty of them are publicly traded.

Challenges of building an IPO-ready company

At first glance, it makes little sense that IPOs are so rare in the security industry. The facts we hear about the industry suggest that the opposite should be true:

- Loss amounts from security breaches have been climbing non-stop over the past several decades, and there are no signs that this trend is going to reverse anytime soon.
- Security spending is going up, and even during economic downturns there appears to be no serious reduction of resources deployed on security.
- Small and medium businesses that have historically been able to avoid investing in security, are starting to realize the importance of strengthening their defenses.
- Given the ever-expanding threat landscape, increasing connectivity, adoption of the cloud, and the rise of work-from-anywhere arrangements, to name a few, as well as the professionalization of cybercrime, it is apparent that the impact of security incidents and their frequency is only going to grow.

While all these factors are pointing to an incredible opportunity, the full picture is much more complex.

First and foremost, although security is a growing market, it is a relatively small part of the enterprise IT spend, anywhere between 6-10%, depending on the source we choose to rely on. Security spending does not directly help companies to make more money, and is therefore seen as a cost center and a "necessary evil". Moreover, because improvements to the organization's security posture are hard to test, quantify, and justify, it is unlikely that the share of security spend as a percentage of the IT budget is going to grow significantly beyond where it is today.

Second, the industry is highly fragmented and even the largest vendors own a single digit of the total security market. In my view, the biggest reason why this is the case is the critical role trust plays in product adoption. To do what they are designed to do, security tools require the highest degree of access and trust: customers are required to deploy them in their production environments, share their most sensitive data, and give access to the most confidential parts of the business. Moreover, trust has geopolitical and national boundaries: for example, a business in the US will always prefer to share its sensitive data with a security company based in US, while a company in France will choose to work with a vendor from their own country even though both nations are members of NATO and closely collaborate in the matters of national security. Another factor that slows the adoption of new ideas in security is the fact that the industry is fast-changing, and the mass market tends to be years behind in understanding what threats and attack vectors deserve attention, and what effective approaches to handling them look like.

Combined, these two factors lead to slow sales cycles, and as a second order of consequences, trigger the creation of tens of "me too" vendors all trying to do the same thing. When a new company develops a unique idea or approach, it will usually take time until the market understands its significance and starts to adopt the solution. While the original inventors are investing money to educate prospects about the problem, tens of copycats pop up selling to slightly different markets, geographies, or customer groups, or offering a variation of the same products. This means that none of the players can move fast and after a year or two, own the majority of the market, be it in the US or globally.

Although not too long ago a company could go public solely based on the hype and projections of future growth, today that is no longer enough. A startup getting ready to an IPO needs to be able to get to at least $100 million in annual recurring revenue and show a strong year-over-year growth trend. When blitzscaling (growing very fast) is not possible, the only way this can be done is by offering a suite of solutions, or in other words, a platform.

Building a platform means picking a vertical or a problem area within security, and solving a set of problems in that area so that instead of choosing many separate solutions, enterprise buyers would buy one product. The reason this is hard is because an entry point to building a platform must still be a point solution - a tool that solves one tightly scoped problem well. And, because nearly every startup that starts as a narrowly focused product has an ambition to grow into a platform, it becomes apparent that only a few, very few, will be able to make it. To make the situation worse, many segments of the security market do not have a total addressable market large enough to ever exceed the $100 million ARR

- a revenue threshold companies planning to an IPO are typically being benchmarked against.

It is entirely possible that a startup can become one out of a thousand and successfully go public. But, if we are being realistic, for most companies the only possible way to generate return on investment for their founders, employees, angels, and VCs is getting acquired.

Three types of acquisitions

In the tech industry, there are three types of acquisitions:

- Business acquisitions.
- Product acquisitions.
- Talent acquisitions, often called "acqui-hiring".

If a company can establish a strong product-market fit, build a sustainable business model, and find a way to continue growing, it may generate interest from a strategic buyer who would like to add it to its portfolio. This kind of acquisition is called "business acquisition" because the buyer is looking to purchase a well-functioning business with a good product, stellar team, and strong distribution. M&A transactions that fall under this category come at the largest price tag of several millions or even billions of dollars and are quite rare.

There are cases when a startup was able to build a great product, but for different reasons struggled to turn it into a successful business. Large security companies with well-established distribution channels are often on the lookout for products they can add to their portfolio and sell by leveraging the parent company's salesforce. Many buyers of security products are platform players looking for new components they can integrate with the main solution. Product acquisitions can generate good returns, although as a rule, they are significantly lower compared to business-driven M&As.

The last type is talent acquisition, often called "acqui-hiring". Talent acquisitions happen when the company has assembled a rockstar team but is unable to build a leading product and a business around it. Acqui-hiring makes the most sense if the team has developed some unique skills in the new, cutting-edge field that are hard to find on the open market. Talent acquisitions are typically announced in a brief press release; the transaction amount is often not disclosed (it can be quite low).

From the outside, it is usually very hard to tell which company is acquired for what reasons, although experienced market insiders can typically guess it pretty accurately by looking at different signals. Moreover, being acquired is not at all a sign of startup success: many acquisitions don't make any money for founders, employees, and investors. This is especially the case with talent acquisitions.

Cybersecurity buyers and their motivations

Not every buyer is driven by the same motivations and has the same plans for companies they acquire. Broadly, there are four main types of acquirers active in the cybersecurity space: security product companies, security service companies, tech companies outside of security, and private equity (PE) firms.

Cybersecurity product companies typically buy other product startups. Acquisitions of service providers by product companies are rare. When they do happen, it is usually driven by the need to hire hard-to-find, specialized talent so that the business can design and subsequently upsell its existing customers on hands-on, premium offerings. An example would be an endpoint security company looking to build an in-house incident response (IR) capability they can layer on top of their base product.

There are several reasons why a product company would want to acquire another product startup, including adding a new revenue source to its portfolio, expanding the capabilities of its platform, or entering a new market. Sometimes, these decisions are motivated by the need to remain relevant: large, slow-moving enterprises may find it hard to develop new, innovative capabilities in-house, so an acquisition might be a great way to solve the problem.

Since the main asset of security service providers is people, and hiring good people is incredibly hard, buying other service companies is the only scalable way for service firms to grow their teams. Another unique factor that causes them to constantly look for new acquisition targets is the need to expand in new markets. In services, reputation and relationships are everything, and adding a known, established services provider to the service firm's portfolio is a good way to quickly expand its presence in new geographies.

Service providers rarely buy security product vendors; when it happens, it is typically a sign that they are either looking to go public, and think that adding a product to their portfolio will increase their valuation multiples (that is usually the case), or they are exploring a strategic shift of their business. They could be planning to raise venture funding (VCs prefer to fund product or product-enabled companies), improve unit economics and achieve scale by automating manual tasks, or provide a visibility layer for their customers.

Although in the past we haven't seen many examples of technology companies outside of security buying product and service security vendors, that has started to change in recent years. It is hard to generalize about the motivations or the outcomes of these kinds of acquisitions as they are few and far between, and each one seems to be fairly unique. Some tech companies have accumulated large amounts of data and their leadership is looking for ways to capitalize on this factor by designing new offerings of which security is one of the obvious choices. Adding security capabilities as an additional value-add alongside core products, and gaining access to hard-to-find security talent are the two factors that, in my view, are going to increase the number of cybersecurity acquisitions by tech companies.

Lastly, it is worth briefly discussing another type of acquirer of security products and services that has emerged as a strong contender in the M&A space - private equity firms, or PEs. Private equity is a unique type of buyer that acquires companies it believes are undervalued so that it can achieve operational efficiency and sell them later at a higher price.

Private equity firms focus on buying established product and service vendors and have little interest in startups in search of the product-market fit. For the transaction to move forward, the PE firm's partners must believe the company will be worth more after they make changes to how it's run and what it does. These changes typically include combining several products into a large platform, merging multiple service providers into one, restructuring the company, reducing costs and achieving operational efficiency, changing the company leadership, and embarking on large-scale integrations, to name some. Some segments of the industry see a high concentration of PE-owned security companies, in particular identity products and security service providers.

It is worth noting that even if the startup isn't a market leader, as long as it's solving a real problem well, it can be bought. Multiple variables come into play, including the quality of the team, the reputation of the product among customers, how much money the company has raised, and what its current valuation looks like. To be interesting to buyers, startups should look to grow quickly but not rush into a "unicorn" valuation as that increases the chances that the company will get too expensive and therefore won't be seen as an attractive target.

Expert Insight

"Private equity's footprint in the cybersecurity sector has expanded significantly, with PE firms now responsible for about half of the M&A transactions, frequently outcompeting strategic buyers. For shareholders, engaging with a PE for a majority recap (aka buyout) provides a tactical avenue for a partial exit. This move not only allows founders to monetarily safeguard personal gains but also offers investors a chance to secure a portion of their returns, reducing overall exposure. Moreover, it leaves room for potential future gains without facing a binary, all-or-nothing outcome. This strategy allows stakeholders to continue participating in the company's growth, aiming for a larger payoff in the future, a 'second bite at the apple' if you will."

- Dino Boukouris, Founder and Managing Partner at Altitude Cyber

Expert Insight

"Despite the hype and headlines, large exits in cybersecurity don't happen very often — you just hear about them when they do. From 2021-2023, 80 percent of exits in the cybersecurity industry have been for $250 million or less. Nearly 50 percent have been under $100 million. The average price of disclosed acquisitions is $77 million, and likely lower if undisclosed prices were known. Unicorns are exceptionally rare: only 64 cybersecurity companies have ever exited for $1 billion or higher. All this data is publicly available in reports released by Momentum Cyber."

- Cole Grolmus, Founder and Author at Strategy of Security

Deep Dive

To learn more about how to think about exits in cybersecurity, check out a Venture in Security deep dive titled "Raising capital and understanding paths to an exit: thoughts and mental models for cybersecurity startup founders". You can find it by navigating to https://ventureinsecurity.net/p/raising-capital-and-understanding or by scanning this QR code.

SECTION 3

Trends shaping the future of the cybersecurity industry

Moving from promise-based to evidence-based security

In the past few decades, business has been moving from activities-driven to outcome-driven approaches in everything from marketing and sales to product, engineering, human resources, and arguably any other functional area. In practical terms, this means that sales teams are focused on reaching their quota, product teams are optimizing for monthly active users (MAU), annual recurring revenue (ARR), and several other metrics while marketing tracks conversions and engagement. There is a lot to be said about the so-called vanity metrics, but the important fact remains true: instead of being asked "What are you doing?", business leaders are expected to explain what outcomes they are achieving and why it matters. Until very recently, security has remained one of the few functional areas with generally unknown return on investment. However, as businesses are starting to look for ways to measure the ROI of their security investments, security is forced to catch up with other functional areas.

Over the past several years, we have seen a growing number of organizations starting to move from promise-based to evidence-based security. Instead of treating security as a tool selection problem ("What do I need to buy to be secure?"), more and more businesses are starting to think about it more holistically, looking for ways to future-proof their security programs by operationalizing MITRE ATT&CK® and other frameworks, benchmarking their controls against industry best practices, hiring security engineers to build custom-tailored solutions and automate manual processes, adopting test-driven, continuous security approaches, and the like.

Mature security professionals know that security is a process, not a feature. The best way to build a security posture is to build it on top of controls and infrastructure that can be observed, tested, and enhanced. It is not built on promises from vendors that must be taken at face value. This means that the exact set of malicious activity and behavior the company is protected from should be known and security teams should be able to test and prove this. It also means that if security practitioners can describe something they want to detect and prevent, they should be able to apply it unilaterally without vendor intervention. For example, if a security engineer has read about WannaCry, they should have the ability to create their own detection logic without waiting a day or two until their vendor does a new release.

Moving from promise-based to evidence-based security shifts the ownership from third parties to security teams. When the board asks a CISO – "The whole industry is talking about the log4j vulnerability – are we protected?", it most certainly doesn't want to hear "I don't know, hopefully our vendor will take care of that". The CISO should be able to say "This is the security coverage we have in place for log4j. This is how it is detected, and this is the action we are taking to address it". The ability to control one's own destiny is becoming more and more critical as every environment today is unique. An experienced security engineer who knows their organization's business processes can think of many behaviors specific to their company that are critical to detect or prevent. It has become common knowledge that commercial vendors cannot develop out-of-the-box coverage against every single threat simply because that would greatly increase the number of false positives, and they cannot afford to build logic that can only be used by 0.001% of their customers.

Founders building solutions for enterprise customers should be prepared to answer questions about how their products are working. Mature security teams are starting to look for tools that provide them with visibility and control over their environment, and allow them to customize generic solutions to their specific needs, not simply use some "secret sauce" to "keep them safe". While vendors are and will continue to be expected to do the hard work, more and more buyers will be demanding the ability to look under the hood and understand the approach the company is taking to ensure their security.

Expert Insight

"Security is really a data science: controls, whether preventative or alerting, are based on data. But, where do we get the data to drive these insights? The Threat, which is where MITRE ATT&CK has provided the periodic table to describe these elements of an attack campaign in a common vernacular. This leads beyond just evidence-based insights, it's the critical process driving 'detection engineering' that provides the business and operational context to make your defensive stack actually yours."

- Bryson Bort, Founder and CEO at SCYTHE, Founder and Chairman at GRIMM Cyber

Deep Dive

To learn more about this trend, check out a Venture in Security deep dive titled "Future of cyber defense and move from promise-based to evidence-based security". You can find it by navigating to https://ventureinsecurity.net/p/future-of-cyber-defense-and-move or by scanning this QR code.

Evolution of channel partners

In the past, the process of implementing a security program in an organization was somewhat sequential: a company would develop a security strategy with the help of a consultancy, purchase security solutions with the assistance from a VAR, hire an integrator to get it all together, and choose to engage an MSSP for the ongoing monitoring. This model no longer holds because every type of channel partner, regardless of their main area of expertise, wants to own the full customer journey.

Consultancy firms that have previously focused on strategy, have now built deep technical capabilities enabling them to play the role of integrators and service providers. This shift is expected: as security is becoming increasingly more technical and complex, it is not realistic that someone without recent practical experience in the field can develop a comprehensive cyber defense strategy. Consulting companies that were once known as PowerPoint shops where new MBA grads would come up with cookie-cutter solutions to hard problems have turned into powerhouses of technical security talent.

More and more software is moving to the SaaS model, and tools and configurations that previously required many months of development are being provisioned and deployed in a relatively short amount of time. The adoption of everything-as-code is making it even easier to transfer configurations from one environment to another. As the integration work that would previously take two to three years to complete can be done within a few months, system integrators are being forced to either increase the volume of their existing services or introduce new ones. Acquiring more customers in today's competitive environment is harder than retaining existing ones, hence system integrators are actively turning into holistic security providers as well.

The value-added reseller (VAR) model is being threatened the most. The rise of SaaS, direct sales and marketplaces, have shaken the dominance of this once-important player in the market. Now, the effects of data gravity are reshaping the distribution channels entirely, turning platforms of Google, Microsoft, Amazon, and Snowflake, to name a few, into the sellers of security solutions. With the ever-decreasing number of stand-alone security vendors for VARs to sell, those that want to remain in the game a decade or two from now, need to pivot their business models from selling somebody else's products to selling their own security expertise.

As consulting firms, system integrators, value-add resellers, and MSSPs are all trying to do everything at once, the lines between their areas of expertise continue to blur. A natural conclusion is that the consolidation we have been seeing in the past few years will keep progressing, and a decade from now there will be no such thing as VARs or system integrators - only full-stack security service providers capable of helping customers with all of their needs in one place.

One of the factors accelerating the emergence of full-stack security providers is that customers do not want to deal with handoffs. If Deloitte develops the security strategy, Optiv handles the integration of tools, and Capgemini takes on the managed services part, handoffs between parties become unnecessarily complex. Customers are looking for one-stop solutions, offered by providers that are both strategic and deeply technical, capable of operating with them across the entire security lifecycle. In the future, security service providers who will survive the competitive market, will be seen as trusted advisors and will have to add value on top of tooling they didn't choose by understanding the business, the risks in the customer's environment, and establishing systems and processes, to address unique risks of the organizations they serve.

Founders building products that target enterprise customers should recognize that although the nature of the channel is changing, its role, at least for the next decade, is not likely to decrease (in fact, the opposite is true). Although entrepreneurs should certainly be looking at new ways to distribute their offerings, they must remember that more than $9 out of every $10 of cybersecurity sold to the enterprise market is done via channel partners. This alone, combined with the fact that a large percentage of Fortune 500 companies buy tooling exclusively through channel, should be a strong argument to prioritize this distribution method.

Rise of the data gravity effect

The idea of data gravity was first introduced in 2010 by Dave McCrory, a software engineer who observed that as more and more data is gathered in one place, it "builds mass". That mass attracts services and applications, and the larger the amount of data, the greater its gravitational pull, meaning the more services and applications will be attracted to it and the more quickly that will happen.

Data gravity leads to the tectonic shift in cybersecurity: security data is moving to Snowflake, BigQuery, Microsoft Azure Data Warehouse, Amazon Security Lake, Amazon Redshift, Databricks, and the like. As the amount of data increases in size, moving it around to various applications becomes hard and costly. Snowflake, Google, Amazon, and Microsoft understand their advantage incredibly well and are taking action to fully leverage it by pursuing the "land and expand" strategy: getting customers to adopt the product for one use case, and once the data is in, start offering other products and services.

Platform companies grow their ecosystem with one or more of the three reasons in mind:

- Acquisition - make it very easy for potential customers to integrate with their existing and preferred tech stack so that they are more likely to adopt the platform.
- Retention - get the customer super deep into the platform's ecosystem so that the cost of switching to another solution becomes prohibitively high.
- Monetization - generate revenue from the platform usage.

We are still early enough in the shift to the cloud, and all major cloud providers are fighting to be chosen as the number one solution with the understanding that the future is shaping up to be multi-cloud. Because the fight for the cloud market share is still being waged, the focus of cloud providers is predominantly on the first two goals - acquisition and retention.

For as long as there is aggressive competition for the cloud market share, the main area of focus for major cloud providers is horizontal expansion (acquiring new customers and getting them as deep as possible into their ecosystem). As soon as the speed of public cloud adoption slows down (and we know it will), cloud providers will be faced with the need to sustain their revenue growth. This is when the vertical expansion will start and looking for ways to monetize the data of their existing customers will likely be the natural first step in that direction. It is during this monetization part that I expect that cloud providers will attempt to address more and more security use cases in-house. As cloud offerings become more commoditized, cloud providers might start doing more security as a way to differentiate. Granted, there are other areas they could be looking at first, such as data analytics, infrastructure automation, and other use cases where they can add a lot of value without increasing their liability exposure.

In the next decade, data platform providers have the potential to grow into the largest distribution channel for cybersecurity. Security companies capable of getting their foot in the door and building partnerships can sell their offerings entirely through this channel. Field sales representatives for data lakes and cloud providers, equipped with marketing collateral and information about cybersecurity solutions, can upsell and cross-sell to their existing customer base with little effort. Data warehouses and cloud providers track two metrics: storage and consumption, or to put it differently - storing the data, and ensuring that customers use as many add-ons and services as possible, fully leveraging the capabilities of the platform. Selling cybersecurity on top of their core offerings can drive consumption, help sales reps hit their quotas, and provide startups with steady streams of revenue.

Expert Insight

"As I understand it, ingesting and consuming is really a matter of storage and computing. All platforms mentioned understand that computing is more important than storage. Storage is becoming increasingly commoditized, while computing is the scarce resource. Bringing compute to the data instead of moving the data around will be de-facto standard architecture (which poses an interesting but obvious innovator dilemma - making money

out of compute is a lot more profitable than copying data and making money out of storage). When you apply all the above to security analytics, offloading data management to a third party means security vendors can focus on the 'race to the top' and actual security instead of building another log management tool while enjoying the absolute best price-performance optimization (it's going to be very hard to impossible for security vendors, SIEM included to compete with cloud service providers and data warehouses on that)."

- Uri May, Co-Founder and CEO at Hunters

Expert Insight

"Security data lakes have been around for a while, but they've only recently become relevant outside of the banking/tech one-percenters. Cybersecurity startups have played a key role in democratizing what used to require a big team of in-house developers and data scientists. The most successful of these startups used partnerships to turn the platform providers, with their thousands of sellers and huge customer base, into force-multipliers for the startup sales team. While the platform provider likely lacks the expertise in the startup's use case, a collaborative effort can unlock for security organizations the dramatic savings and risk reduction potential of cloud data platforms. Rising data gravity will accelerate this process."

- Omer Singer, security strategist at Snowflake and Anvilogic

---

Deep Dive

To learn more about this trend, check out a Venture in Security deep dive titled "Game of Thrones in cybersecurity: data gravity, industry consolidation, platform play, private equity, and the great cyber gold rush". You can find it by navigating to https://ventureinsecurity.net/p/game-of-thrones-in-cybersecurity or by scanning this QR code.

Rise of security engineering

In the past decade, we have been seeing a big push towards adopting an engineering approach in all areas of security.

This shift originated in cloud-first product organizations, where software engineering principles and practices now underpin how infrastructure is provisioned, how security policies and configurations are applied, how the company's security posture is tested and measured, and how changes to security configurations are implemented and tracked. While DevOps engineers are in charge of provisioning and managing the infrastructure, security engineers that combine a strong knowledge of engineering with a deep understanding of security are ideally suited to secure it.

Most cybersecurity professionals today developed their skills in IT, designing network architectures, provisioning firewalls and managing firewall policies, and keeping the IT in the enterprise going. Unfortunately, many of the people in charge of security have only the most basic understanding of software engineering, preventing them from developing the skills they need in a world where everything including infrastructure, policies, and detections, exists as code. It makes perfect sense that when the underlying infrastructure is in code, security professionals should be able to read and write code. The same is true for automation and the use of APIs: since the vast majority of technical tasks are now accomplished at scale via APIs (including the work that was previously done manually within security teams themselves), we need people who understand how to design, use, and securely decommission APIs.

Security engineering teams are expected to go beyond operational controls building engineering solutions to security problems. As more and more organizations realize that off-the-shelf security tools often do not address the uniqueness of their needs and environments, those that have the right resources and support to take hardening their security posture seriously are going beyond configuring commercial products. While for some use cases, a tool purchased from a security vendor can be suited to implement as is, more often than not it needs some tweaking to accommodate the unique needs of an organization. We also see an ever-growing understanding, especially among large enterprises handling a lot of data and cloud-native companies, that commercial tools are not able to address the multitude of security needs and requirements. These companies are starting to build some elements of their security stack in-house, delegating the design and development of these solutions to internal security architects and security engineers.

Tom Tovar, CEO and co-creator of Appdome, suggested in one of his podcasts that we can put security organizations into three categories:

- Traditional security teams, composed of technically strong security professionals with deep knowledge of security and compliance, and best practices for both.
- Advanced security teams that often have security researchers and security architects tasked with designing systems, product evaluation, penetration testing, etc.
- Cybersecurity and engineering organizations that have "hardcore" engineering talent capable of building and delivering security solutions for modern organizations.

I see these categories not as different stages of maturity, but as an evolution in terms of organizational needs. Cloud-native companies are starting to build security engineering teams designed to work closely with DevOps, software engineering, and product development. With that, many of the elements that would traditionally be owned by IT and security teams, are now owned by DevOps and security engineering teams. This model that relies on builders - engineering talent able to craft security solutions - is not needed for every organization. However, as more and more companies are built cloud-first from day one, as their environments are becoming more unique with the proliferation of SaaS tools, and as more security teams realize the shortcomings of adopting products out of the box, we will see a massive shift towards security engineering.

As of today, best practices for organizational design have not caught up with the rise of security engineering. First, while security engineering teams have their own tools they are responsible for managing, there seem to be many conflicts around ownership between security engineers and software/DevOps engineers as well as operational security teams. Organizational conflicts and unclear areas of ownership are natural steps in the formation of any new discipline, so what we are seeing is normal and expected.

Founders of cybersecurity companies should keep in mind that although engineering-centric organizations may be more exciting to work with, the reality is that companies able to afford to hire the "hardcore" engineering talent represent a very small percentage of the market. Moreover, security teams at these enterprises are well-resourced and more than comfortable building their own tools. A security startup with an ambition to grow into a large company, should keep the size of the total addressable market in mind and look for solutions that can be adopted by both traditional and modern security teams.

Expert Insight

"There are two advantages to security engineering teams. First is context. Security engineers typically sit within the engineering organization and will have the necessary context to build solutions that solve the core security issue. This leads to faster feedback loops. Moreover, these engineers are also able to properly reason about and influence design tradeoffs to create systems that are beneficial to both engineering and security.

This leads to the second advantage, which is scale. Engineers are able to build solutions that can properly scale rather than just focusing on auditing and monitoring, which require scaling with analysts. This is especially useful in modern infrastructure as development cycles and consequently threats have become faster and more complex in nature. The technical abilities of security engineers can lead to a more symbiotic relationship between security and engineers where security is seen as a value add rather than a cost center."

- Frank Wang, Lead Security Engineer at Headway and author of the Frankly Speaking blog

---

Expert Insight

"Organizations typically do a buy vs. build analysis when they need a solution. The 'buy' case should capture the required features, the likelihood the analyzed vendors will support them, and subscription cost. The 'build' case should include necessary resources, building time, and total maintenance cost.

Organizations typically prefer to buy when their needs are captured well in a commercial product, and the cost tradeoff is reasonable. Organizations prefer to build when the market for their problem is immature, their needs are bespoke, and/or their engineering cost is very high."

- Travis McPeak, Co-Founder and CEO at Resourcely

Deep Dive

To learn more about the reasons why cybersecurity of the future will look a lot like software engineering, check out a Venture in Security deep dive titled "The rise of security engineering and how it is changing the cybersecurity of tomorrow". You can find it by navigating to https://ventureinsecurity.net/p/the-rise-of-security-engineering or by scanning this QR code.

Growing role of security practitioners in the buying process

While founders, product leaders, and marketers are arguing whether or not product-led growth is going to transform the way security products are purchased, more and more CISOs are starting to delegate tool evaluation to people on their teams.

There are several reasons why this is happening. First, the number of vendors in each category makes it impossible to assess every single option available on the market. Second, CISOs have too much on their plate - they are focused on defining the security strategy, growing teams, building relationships with other departments, working with the board and peers from the leadership, and ensuring compliance with the ever-expanding list of regulations. The only way to keep up with the growing demands of the role is to build strong high-performing teams and delegate more. Third, as the government is forcing CISOs to defend their decisions in a court of law, the need to reduce liability and ensure an unbiased vendor evaluation process is going to become even stronger. As more security leaders are facing charges ranging from negligence to fraud and concealing material facts from the regulators, the pressure to have a solid paper trail for every product and vendor choice is going to grow, and with that so will the role of security teams in these decisions.

There are typically two ways in which security practitioners get involved in vendor selection. The more common one, the top-down method, is when CISOs provide security practitioners with a shortlist of products to evaluate. The shortlist is typically based on the CISO's research as well as feedback from peers, and recommendations from industry analysts, consulting firms, resellers, integrators, and investors. In the case of bottom-up recommendations, the initial evaluation of tools and proof of value is coming from those doing the work. After verifying that the solution could be well-suited to address the organization's needs, security practitioners recommend it to their management.

While security leaders are and will continue to be the approvers of the buying decisions and the owners of the budget, I anticipate that we will be seeing the role of individual contributors in the buying process grow. This makes sense since technical individual contributors are keeping track of emerging threats, continuously testing new approaches in their home labs, and evaluating new products. Security practitioners are spending their free time on security Discords, attending BSides and DEF CON events, and constantly exchanging learnings about what is happening on the ground with their peers. This means that while CISOs maintain a solid holistic view of business risks, to understand what vulnerabilities are being exploited and what attack vectors the company should be paying attention to, they will need to involve those doing the actual work - security practitioners.

Another reason for delegating the tool evaluation to practitioners is the need to build empowered security teams. Similar to how software development has evolved from top-down directives to enabling individual engineers to own their work, security teams are inevitably going to change the way the work is structured and distributed. More and more security leaders are looking for ways to build high-performing teams, capable of assessing the needs of the organization and evaluating the tools that can solve those needs. Lastly, security leaders are drowning in spam and never-ending requests from vendors to "get a demo". Instead of triaging vendor requests and deciding whom to have a call with, it's wiser to start by soliciting ideas from the team, and only then prioritizing which products to evaluate.

To increase the chances of winning deals in this new environment, founders need to change the way they build their products. First and foremost, security practitioners should be able to get started with the product without having to go through a lengthy sales and qualification process. Second, practitioner-focused security tooling needs to be built on the principle of interoperability. Users should be allowed to own and fully control their data, and freely decide what type of data is sent and where. Security providers should as much as possible use common taxonomies, standards, frameworks, and protocols to make integrating with other products easy. Moreover, users of security tools should be given a generic way to integrate with providers that are not a part of the vendor's network of partners, instead of locking them into the ecosystem of "approved" and "preferred" options. Third, security teams should be able to customize tooling to fit their needs, which often means leveraging APIs, architecture workflows, and complex integrations, all of which should not be an afterthought for vendors. Fourth, security solutions should be testable, scalable, transparent, and easy to navigate.

Expert Insight

"While still uncommon, founders should relentlessly pursue relationships with field practitioners early in the ideation process and maintain these connections throughout the product's journey. This is especially crucial in cybersecurity. Often, tools are chosen by the CISO with limited input from practitioners, yet these individuals are the ultimate end-users. A tool's user-friendliness and its ability to streamline the practitioner's work are pivotal. At renewal time, if the product falls short, the CISO faces a tough decision: discard an ineffective tool to support the team or retain it, risking employee attrition. Engaging practitioners early can mitigate such dilemmas."

- Ofir Har-Chen, Co-Founder and CEO at a stealth-mode cybersecurity startup

Blurring boundaries between products and services

A decade ago, anyone looking to segment and classify cybersecurity companies would first split them into two buckets: products and services.

Service companies are the ones that sell professional expertise. Security service providers typically have three lines of business: reselling products, project-based services (penetration testing, security assessments, and the like), and managed services (24/7

SOC and continuous security monitoring, detection, and response). Because of the linear relationship between growth and the need to hire more people and few barriers to entry, service companies have seen lower exit multiples compared to their product counterparts, and consequently, they struggled to attract venture funding.

Product companies make money by developing, marketing, and selling a product. After the product is built, it can be efficiently sold en masse to its entire addressable market. This is not available to service providers who are repeating the same (or similar) work for different clients, often starting from scratch every time. This made it possible for product companies to achieve economies of scale, rapidly acquire new customers, and capture a large percentage of the market share quickly. Product companies can bring outsized returns and are therefore well-suited for venture funding.

The line between cybersecurity products and services is becoming very blurry; as we go into the future, this line will likely disappear altogether. More and more buyers are looking for holistic solutions that fully address their problems. They don't purchase a product or a service, they purchase an outcome. It's then up to a vendor how it delivers the outcome - by offering a product, a service, or a combination of both.

A leading factor that drives security product vendors to offer services is the desire to increase their share of the customer wallets, and subsequently generate more revenue. Designing services that can be sold as value-added or premium versions of the offering can be especially successful for a few reasons. First, not everyone is looking for the same level of service, which naturally creates opportunities for more tailored solutions. Second, there is a growing realization that products alone can only do so much and that skilled security practitioners are required to achieve an advantage over the adversary. Third, it is not currently possible to automate or fully productize incident response, so a security vendor looking to provide holistic coverage to its customers often has little choice but to find a way to offer a service component.

Service providers also have strong reasons to develop product offerings.

The economics of the service model doesn't offer a well-understood path for building and scaling a tech company quickly. First, because of the high reliance on expensive talent, the typical margins a well-managed security service provider can achieve are around 40-60%, significantly below that of a product company which can go well above 80%. Second, a product company can hire, and if needed replace its employees much more easily than a service firm. In cybersecurity, good talent is scarce so a service company's ambitions for hyper-growth will always be limited by the supply of security practitioners. These factors impact the economics of mergers and acquisitions: exit multiples of security service companies are substantially lower than those of their product counterparts. When and if a security service provider is considering going public, it will typically try acquiring (or more rarely, building in-house) a product component. Having a product side of the business can increase the amount of money the firm stands to raise during the IPO. The same is true for acquisitions: everything else being equal, a service provider with a product will be valued higher than the one without. Although there are other factors that compel service providers to offer products, the economic motivator is by far the strongest reason why they are moving in this direction.

Expert Insight

"Founders building a security company should understand what this trend means in their space, and consider how a hybrid approach could be leveraged to overcome the talent demands of a service offering and the knowledge shortcomings of pure products. Adding a thin layer of human-expertise atop a highly-tuned automated collection and analysis system may deliver the ideal outcome to your customers (efficacy and quality), investors (efficiency and scalability), and business goals (growth and retention)."

- Kyle Hanslovan, Co-Founder and CEO at Huntress

Expert Insight

"Back in the day, security practitioners would say 'You need people, processes, and technology to succeed'; this statement is still true today. So, why don't companies bring all three ingredients together? If they do the right thing and build a service component, then they do not get funded as much or at all. Cybersecurity companies built today are designed to optimize not for what actually solves the problem, but what produces the highest returns for investors. Unintentionally, the cybersecurity industry has turned into big pharma: instead of focusing on solving the root cause of the problem, we do what makes us the most money. Most buyers of cybersecurity solutions are unsophisticated, meaning we can tell them we will monitor, detect, and respond, then offer them incident response services when they get hacked. That is three revenue streams compared to one of actually implementing and managing the proper controls to get a company secure. The cybersecurity industry is still in the infancy phase, and as it matures, there will be no line between the products and services."

- Corey White, Founder and CEO at Cyvatar

Deep Dive

To learn more about this trend, check out a Venture in Security deep dive titled "Enmeshment in cybersecurity: blurring boundaries between products and services". You can find it by navigating to https://ventureinsecurity.net/p/enmeshment-in-cybersecurity-blurring or by scanning this QR code.

Deep Dive

To learn more about the reasons why VCs tend to stay away from funding service companies and why they could benefit from doing it regardless, check out a Venture in Security deep dive titled "A deep look at investing in cybersecurity services for VCs: why, why not, and how to". You can find it by navigating to https://ventureinsecurity.net/p/a-deep-look-at-investing-in-cybersecurity or by scanning this QR code.

Blurring boundaries between open source and closed source

Open source isn't just another attack vector; it is a foundation of cybersecurity as we know it. Hacking was built in communities of people sharing their knowledge for free, without any agenda or expectations of a payoff. Decades later, we are spending millions of dollars on defense yet the attackers often use the same open source tools built 15 years ago without having to spend a dime.

Over the past two decades, the nature of open source has changed dramatically. A case in point is Microsoft which evolved from calling open source "cancer" in 2001, to becoming one of the world's leading contributors since 2017 as measured by the number of employees actively contributing to open source. A decade ago, most open source projects were driven by individuals with very few companies present in the space, and even fewer being able to generate revenue from their offerings. Although some projects that started small, over time evolved into large companies such as Elastic, most did not have any commercial components or aspirations. Today, open source is very familiar to people and organizations across the globe. Tech companies routinely open source their internal initiatives, use open source tools themselves, and support projects that align with their vision financially. Industry-wide advances such as infrastructure-as-code and detections-as-code were accelerated by both passionate individuals sharing their contributions in the open, and large corporations allowing their work to become public.

As years passed, the line between open source and commercial offerings started to blur. For example, while open source projects of the past had a distinct "open source look" and required a lot of effort to get started, the user experience of many open source tools today is indistinguishable from that of their commercial counterparts. The biggest shift, however, has to do with the fact that there are now many ways to make money with open source. In the past, security enthusiasts built open source on the side, using their main job to finance this side "hobby". Today, more and more open source founders are finding ways to focus on their creations full-time - whether it's through designing business models that unlock revenue streams, signing up for GitHub sponsors and establishing partnership arrangements with corporations, or even getting hired by large companies such as Microsoft to work on open source.

Two decades ago, open source was seen solely as a way of building products and sharing interesting ideas at no cost. Today, a lot of open source is regarded as an effective tool for commercial enterprises to boost demand generation and design highly effective business models. We are starting to see more open source cybersecurity tools offering a freemium model where customers pay more for scale, cloud hosting, or more advanced versions of the product. Instead of relying on donations and sponsorship, open source founders are starting to design ways to generate revenue reliably so that they can scale and grow their product as their main area of focus. Some projects go as far as to raise funding from venture capital funds. At the same time, commercial cybersecurity vendors are starting to add open source capabilities to their products, and sometimes even acquire popular open source projects to complement their offerings, or to market to the well-established community of practitioners aligned with the company's target market.

In the coming decade, the line between open source and commercial cybersecurity offerings is going to disappear. More and more companies, regardless of how they were started, will be built using both open source and closed source components in ways that complement one another, and enable startups to both create and capture more value.

Cybersecurity entrepreneurs should think about what parts of their offering should remain proprietary, and which can be open sourced. Early-stage startups can especially benefit from having an open source component: not only can it allow them to build a community passionate about the problem they are solving, but it can also help to close early enterprise customers. Large companies know that new startups are risky and prone to taking shortcuts, so offering users the ability to fully inspect the inner workings of the platform can help gain trust and gather feedback about what should be improved. At the same time, security founders should keep in mind that building a community around open source tools requires a lot of resources, and just because their work is public, it won't automatically lead to traction and viral growth.

Expert Insight

"Making software open source can be an effective strategy for gaining early traction, but this requires genuine commitment and adequate resources. Merely publishing code publicly is insufficient for establishing a market presence. The software must be well-documented, effectively marketed, and user-friendly, enabling users to operate it independently. As a community begins to form around the software, it is advisable to quickly start offering services, such as support contracts. Engaging with customers who have invested even a small amount can yield valuable, honest feedback and insights into real-world requirements."

- Lennart Koopmann, Founder of nzyme, previously Founder of Graylog

Deep Dive

To learn more about open source and its role in cybersecurity, check out a Venture in Security article titled "Open source in cybersecurity: a deep dive". You can find it by navigating to https://ventureinsecurity.net/p/open-source-in-cybersecurity-a-deep or by scanning this QR code.

Demand for go-to-market strategies that respect buyers and users

Although as we have previously seen, direct sales constitute a small percentage of the dollar amount sold to enterprises, it would be an overstatement to say that it's invisible. On the contrary, it is hard to find a security leader or practitioner who would not be deeply disillusioned about the way cybersecurity is sold: through manufacturing fear, uncertainty, doubt, misinformation, and other aggressive and often unethical practices. There are multiple layers to this problem.

The growing competitiveness and commoditization of the cybersecurity market is making it incredibly hard to differentiate and communicate a company's value proposition. This problem isn't unique to our industry, and neither is it the most acute in security: while there are roughly 3,500 cybersecurity vendors (according to the numbers by industry analyst firm IT-Harvest), fintech, for instance, has almost ten times that. What I think is rather special about security is that because of the high reliance on trust in the buying process, and the fact that it has national and geopolitical dimensions, many companies find at least a handful of loyal customers - just enough to stick around for years and sometimes, decades, instead of growing or going out of business fast.

The fact that cybersecurity is a deeply technical discipline often makes it hard for an average marketing professional to understand what their company's product does, let alone how it works or what the significance of certain technical implementations may be. What makes the situation even worse is that many founders are laser-focused on building next-generation products without taking the time to understand if their creations solve a problem somebody is experiencing. And, because there is no clarity around ideal customers and the problem space, companies' go-to-market becomes to "spray and pray": send as many spam emails and make as many cold calls to as many people as possible, hoping that someone will get a demo and sign on the dotted line.

Hundreds of security leaders are taking it to social media to say that enough is enough. They demand that the industry evolve its sales and marketing tactics to those that treat buyers and users with respect, consider their needs, and focus on their success.

For founders, this calls for rethinking the way they approach their go-to-market and building the company in general:

- Instead of falling in love with the solution, they should look for ways to become experts on the problem.
- Instead of being vague about "stopping all threats" and "offering perfect security", they should be clear about what the company does and for whom.
- Instead of playing the so-called "numbers game", they should take time to do their research and only contact prospects that match their company's ideal customer profile.
- Instead of scanning everyone's badges at security conferences and then spamming them with mass email campaigns, they should contact people who match their company's ideal customer profile and who specifically agreed to hear from them.
- Instead of forcing security practitioners to go through a painful process of qualifying to access their product and attending multiple sales demos, they should make it easier for someone to do a proof of value (POV) and evaluate if the company's solution could solve their problem.

The overarching idea is that founders must be willing to put the needs of the buyers first. Needless to say, most decisions are non-binary: it's not about never sending emails, but about reviewing who should be getting them and what is being sent; it's not about not making sales calls, but about reviewing who should be getting them and how it is done; and so on.

Finally, it's worth reminding ourselves that we must be pragmatic, and focus on what drives results, not on what everybody seems to be doing. Spam and other "spray and pray" tactics may be the "numbers game", but in the industry with a limited number of buyers who are all connected, they may be unnecessarily costly games to play.

Expert Insight

"The cybersecurity market has long capitalized on confusion and hype for revenue generation, a practice that urgently needs to end. Marcus Guevara, a colleague and good friend, encapsulates this issue perfectly with a medical analogy: 'Prescription without diagnosis is malpractice.' Essentially, attempting to address a problem without fully understanding it is not only ineffective but has been a cornerstone of vendor strategies for the past decade. This approach is fundamentally flawed, with its ineffectiveness magnified by the overwhelming noise in marketing echo chambers.

Well-informed decision-makers start by comprehending their own organization's threat models and statistical data before considering any purchases. For example, investing in an expensive EDR solution makes little sense if 70% of your incidents involve malicious email attachments; it's clear that your immediate issue lies with email security, not endpoint security. Recognizing the real problems is crucial.

Upon identifying these actual challenges, decision-makers often turn to trusted peers for recommendations on solutions that specifically address these issues. This approach not only provides a 'warm introduction' to a tested and effective solution but also ensures that the product genuinely delivers on its promises in a real-world setting. Let me be clear that I do not consider big advisory services the same as 'trusted peers' as their model is often tainted by vendor influence.

The crux of the matter in cybersecurity marketing isn't just about selling products; it's about integrity in how these products are presented. Vendors should pivot from exploiting fear to educating their audience. The true art lies in honest communication – letting the capabilities and limitations of a product speak for themselves, without the smoke and mirrors of exaggerated claims. In the dense fog of cybersecurity marketing, transparency is the beacon of trust. Vendors need to cut through the haze with clear, straightforward information about what their products can and can't do. This level of honesty doesn't just build credibility; it fosters a foundation of trust that glossy brochures and buzzwords never will.

The ripple effect of misinformation and overhype in cybersecurity is more than just misleading; it's a dangerous distraction. By focusing attention and resources on the wrong threats, these practices don't just dupe customers; they inadvertently create chinks in our collective armor. It's a cycle that undermines the very essence of security.

In a sea of overzealous marketing, there are still beacons of hope. Companies that prioritize transparency, that focus on genuine problem-solving, and that uphold the principle of 'value first' are the unsung heroes of this industry. They prove that success doesn't have to be at odds with ethics, and that in fact, the two can go hand in hand in creating a more secure digital world.

It's high time for a seismic shift in the cybersecurity industry. We need a collective move towards standard practices that emphasize ethical selling, regulatory compliance, and perhaps most importantly, the establishment of industry-wide ethical guidelines. Such changes wouldn't just uplift the market's integrity; they'd pave the way for more sustainable, trust-based customer relationships."

- Eric Capuano, Founder of Recon Infosec

Expert Insight

"I've interviewed hundreds of security practitioners and one common frustration always emerges: many companies are driven purely by the profit, not by the mission of protection. It's ironic, given the industry's purpose. The pressure to prioritize aggressive, short-term financial gains over ethical, sustainable practices, only to appease investors and generate financial returns, damages customer experiences, ruins brands, and stifles career growth.

I'm seeing a budding shift towards a more customer-first approach. More startups are emphasizing practical and prescriptive customer and employee education, leading with curiosity, actively listening, and applying feedback for more predictable growth. Still, there's much room for improvement. Founders and go-to-market teams must consistently foster empathy, authenticity, and commitment to true customer value. Only then can we start to win this war against adversaries."

- Dani Woolf, Founder and CEO of Audience 1st

Deep Dive

To see how some cybersecurity companies built great businesses while also adding value to the community, check out a Venture in Security piece titled "Looking for ways to promote products and services that make cybersecurity a better place: five unique case studies". You can find it by navigating to https://ventureinsecurity.net/p/looking-for-ways-to-promote-products or by scanning this QR code.

Changing demographics of security buyers

One of the biggest yet rarely discussed changes is not only do security buyers want fewer sales calls, but the demographics of who they are is also evolving. We are witnessing that the next generation of security leaders - older millennials - have a different approach to the sales process. Part of this is driven by the difference in how generations consume news, advertising, media, and entertainment more generally. Millennials are mistrustful of traditional establishment authorities and prefer to buy from influencers that feel authentic by their standards. The following factors about millennials and their buying habits are most relevant to cybersecurity founders:

- They discover new solutions through peer communities, social media, and influencers.
- They want to only be contacted when they are interested in evaluating a new solution (the traditional "push" model is being replaced by the new "pull" model).
- They value the ability to find what they are looking for easily, how and when it works for them.
- They value the ability to sign up and try a product on their own, without having to go through lengthy demos and sales negotiations before they decide the product in question could potentially be a solution to their problem.
- They are looking for the ability to make a purchasing decision without a pushy salesperson, or at least they want to be sure they are interested before speaking to someone.
- They need the ability to do a technical deep dive with the vendor and its security team.
- They are taking it to social media to say what they don't want to see in the industry.
- They are calling out specific vendors for their behaviors, and openly promoting tools they find valuable.

The first generation of security leaders built their careers in an environment when security was not seen as a separate profession, and its role in the company was not well understood. Thanks to the tireless work and advocacy of that generation, we've been able to develop various frameworks and methodologies, set out the basics of security regulations, launch educational programs to prepare much-needed talent and establish the foundations of security as a professional discipline. The new generation of security buyers, most of whom are older millennials, are standing on the shoulders of giants. However, they see the world differently and have a different set of technical skills.

Unlike their predecessors who had no one to ask questions and for the most part, had to figure out things on their own, today's security leaders are often members of peer groups - communities of practitioners that regularly exchange ideas and experiences, share their knowledge, and help each other make better decisions. These groups take many shapes. Some are formal not-for-profit clubs and organizations while others function as informal circles of friends, invite-only Slack groups, Discord servers, Signal groups, and even still IRC. Today, when CISOs are evaluating new security tools, they can ask other security leaders about experiences they've had with the vendor, where it came short of their expectations, and if it's worth talking to the company at all.

As generations of buyers change, so will the go-to-market tactics that are effective. These shifts have happened in fields such as software engineering, and are beginning to happen in security.

Monumental shifts like this don't happen overnight. I think that for large enterprises, the changes I am talking about are roughly a decade or two out; for SMBs, they are already underway. This evolution is indeed bringing new, fresh perspectives to the go-to-market strategies in cybersecurity, enabling companies to choose nurturing community over perfect attribution, lead quality over lead quantity, and improving the buyer's journey over pushing its products. Over time, it will likely weaken the influence of industry analysts and maybe even channel partners as we know them now. That said, founders who are starting their companies today, have to recognize that many of the changes they would love to see, are either going to be slow or may not happen at all. A handful of cloud-native companies do not represent the whole industry, the market startups are competing in is not composed of only the power users, and those who go on social media to complain about vendors are still just a loud minority.

The smartest path forward is to build for the future while living in the present. Doing what needs to be done to make the numbers go up and to the right, in a way that respects the buyers, the users, and other industry participants, and aligns the startup's go-to-market efforts with the preferences of their customers. In practical terms, this means looking for shared commons where buyers from different generations meet, and seeking ways to reach different leadership and buying personas.

Expert Insight

"While this is a daunting task, there are various vendors that have been successful in doing so. The keys to successful future building are:

***Have a stellar product/service/solution** - yes, this seems like a given but having an organization that focuses on solving a problem and continuing to do it well for your customers is always number one. They will be your biggest advocates and the first to tell their community that you're not what you purport to be.*

***Building a team of technical individuals** - from the CEO to go-to-market, every individual needs to understand your product and where it fits in the market.*

***Deep education of each buyer's persona** - while each buyer is an individual and has their own likes, dislikes, etc., we must understand at a high level the intricacies of their role and how to best approach a conversation with them.*

***Influencer program** - as noted above, trust around vendors is built in private invite-only Slack groups, Discord servers, Signal groups, and even still IRC. This means that building relationships with those that can influence these conversations is vital.*

***Accountability** - make sure that you are constantly checking that you are accountable to how you want to go-to-market and that it is always in the best benefit of your buyers, not your bottom line."*

- Corin Imai, cybersecurity marketing leader, formerly a security researcher

Expert Insight

"The shift in how different generations consume media and decide how to buy products significantly impacts cybersecurity marketing. Millennials are skeptical of traditional authorities and lean towards peers and authentic influencers on social media rather than advisory firms. Younger buyers are also more values-driven and prioritize companies that align with their political views and ethics. Vendors face the challenge of appealing to a diverse, diffuse, and often polarized marketplace. Recognizing the power of peer recommendations and the influence of professional networks will be crucial to success. Engaging these communities, fostering genuine connections, and encouraging open discussions about products will become more impactful than conventional marketing methods, signifying a shift from traditional top-down sales tactics to a more bottom-up, user-oriented approach."

- Oliver Rochford, product strategy advisor and former Gartner analyst

Rise of security platforms and industry consolidation

It is hard to find a person or a company that would not be convinced that we need fewer security vendors. From security leaders and practitioners to industry analysts, investors, and founders, everyone seems to agree that it is unreasonable that security teams should rely on hundreds of tools to do their jobs. On the vendor side, several large platform companies are fighting for customer wallets, but despite all the aggressive acquisitions and new product launches, none as of the time of writing has been able to capture even 10% of the security market. On the customer side, the push for consolidating security spend is real. So far, Microsoft has been the main company that benefited from the security teams' desire to reduce the number of tools by doubling down on its well-rehearsed strategy of bundling security with its other offerings. We are still early into this trend and it remains to be seen who will come out as a winner in the long term.

Many factors have led us here. First, there is the previously discussed reliance on trust and the fact that it is very hard for a security company to blitzscale and capture a large share of the market quickly. Second, a large number of investors are willing to write checks to security startups, and cyber-focused VCs alone have, according to my calculations, announced $7.5 billion of venture capital dedicated exclusively to cybersecurity in the past decade with ~80% of that committed since 2019. Last but not least, although many founders do have the ambition of building large platform companies, to get a way in they need to start with a smaller, well-defined use case. Of those that find a product-market fit with their initial idea, most struggle to expand into other areas because of how competitive the market has become, and how many of their rivals are trying to execute the same playbook.

What is interesting is that the idea of industry consolidation, or moving from the "best of breed" to "best of suite" tools is not a cybersecurity invention. In every industry, the same two cycles repeat: bundling and unbundling. Here is the oversimplified view of this cycle, and to make it less controversial, I will use an example from marketing, not security. Email marketing has been around for ages, and companies had a way to do it well. Over time, it became apparent that new channels of marketing emerged, and there is more to marketing than sending well-formatted emails. Driven by that realization, more and more founders started launching separate solutions, to help with different aspects of customer outreach, and it didn't take long for marketing teams to end up with a wide variety of disjoint tools not designed to talk to one another. At some point, a visionary entrepreneur comes in, asking "Why don't you consolidate all that into one platform?". Driven by the excitement and the desire to reduce the number of tools, companies replace their stack of products with one solution that solves most of their problems. Over time, since everything tends towards complexity and most large companies fail to preserve their ability to innovate, that one platform solution becomes slow, not performant, and otherwise behind compared to newer alternatives. As new needs emerge and tools that address them well gain traction, the big monolith solution cannot move fast enough to capture these needs. Companies have no choice but to buy many new products from startups. With time, marketing teams once again realize that all their work can no longer be done in one place, and new players appear to consolidate all the flows into one platform.

This cycle, while greatly oversimplified, is both continuous and industry-agnostic. In software engineering, for example, it manifests itself in companies moving from a monolithic engineering stack to microservices, and back to a monolith.

Although bundling and unbundling aren't security-specific, some other trends are.

To understand why we will continue to see a large number of startups, it's worth looking at how the security space operates. We know that bad actors are constantly looking for new ways to accomplish their goals. The number of ways to get in, and hence the number of attack vectors grows every day as new technologies emerge and gain adoption, and new types of vulnerabilities are discovered. No market leader can confidently predict what new attack vector will emerge five years from now. Threat actors are poking holes in hundreds of different directions, but as commercial entities designed to generate profits for their shareholders today, security companies cannot invest their resources to explore all the possibilities trying to both get ahead of everyone else on the market and outsmart the attackers. Leading security vendors need to focus on what's important today, and for the rest, simply wait and see, knowing that there will be someone else who is willing to do this high-risk work.

In parallel, we see thousands of new startups emerge tackling different problems on the market; some are more futuristic than others. Many security professionals pursue approaches and technologies in niche markets that may be too complex or too risky to implement. They know that the chances of failure outweigh the chances of success, but if they do succeed, the payout can be great, and so can the impact on the future of the industry. Microsoft, Palo Alto, and other acquisitive companies can wait, identify the areas of security that matter, and buy one of the top five or ten leaders in that segment. They leave validation to the market knowing that they can always buy a missing piece and integrate it into their core offering later after someone else has already de-risked it.

When new areas of security emerge, they require new skills and perspectives that cannot be easily developed by large companies. For example, the mobile revolution brought the widespread use of a new device that cannot be easily secured by people who built antivirus for Windows. This is why cybersecurity innovation is most often acquired, not built in-house. Both large companies and startup founders benefit from the acquisition-focused cycle of security innovation. Thanks to this cycle, companies can preserve their focus, and wait until they have better information thus de-risking their entry into a new market segment. Founders, on the other hand, take the initial risk knowing that if they are right, they can have a great payout. In the end, it's a win-win.

The industry is, has been, and will continue to consolidate, but this consolidation is a continuous state of security, rather than a process that will be complete over the coming years and magically reduce the number of security startups by 50% or more. The market categories known today are going to consolidate, but then new threats will emerge and with that so will new point solutions, new market categories, more consolidation, new categories, and on and on and on. Eventually, large companies may indeed build enough expertise to tackle emerging areas, but unless they can figure out how to preserve the culture of innovation, they will need to continuously rely on startup acquisitions to stay on top of their game. And, customers will have little choice but to go to early-stage ventures for new, innovative ideas and approaches.

Expert Insight

"One does not build a platform; a platform emerges from the environment where the products exist. What this means is that a startup must build tactically while planning products strategically. Each product must be viable on its own, with customers ready to buy it today. But those products also have to be built with the knowledge they will add up to a platform someday.

This allows you to show growth as a startup today while avoiding technical debt which would make it harder to have a cohesive story around the environment those products live in."

- Maxime Lamothe-Brassard, Co-Founder and CEO at LimaCharlie

SECTION 4

Building cybersecurity companies: a founder's guide

Building a winning team

Cybersecurity founders need industry context

Unlike in some other industries where an outsider can relatively easily find an opportunity and act on it, in cybersecurity, most of the innovation is so technical that it would be very hard for someone without deep domain expertise to make sense of it. This does not mean that a successful founder must be an engineer: what's important is that they can understand the problem, navigate the dynamics of the industry, and be perceived as credible to both buyers and investors. This domain knowledge, credibility, and connections can be achieved in several ways, including by being a security professional, serving in a cyber-focused role in the military, and helping build another cybersecurity company. Founders of most successful cybersecurity companies tend to have different combinations of these backgrounds.

Depending on what the entrepreneurs do before launching a startup, they tend to follow certain patterns. Those coming out of the elite cyber-focused military units and three-letter agencies, tend to have a fantastic understanding of technology, and often a deep experience in offensive security. Moreover, they have an unparalleled advantage compared to their civilian counterparts because a lot of the technologies and methods they were exposed to are years ahead of the commercial industry. What founders that fall under this category often lack are skills around product, sales, marketing, operations, and fundraising. By looking for partners that fill in the gaps, they can form a virtually unstoppable founding team with a high chance of success.

Another group of people who frequently launch their own startups are security practitioners with experience working in mature security teams at cloud-native enterprises, often based in the Bay Area. They are also years ahead of the industry. Security professionals from these backgrounds who become founders have a great network among some of the most forward-thinking security people in the industry on the planet, a good knowledge of what it takes to build a product, and an understanding of the wide variety of the problems that the rest of the industry hasn't faced yet. Founders that fall under this category are similarly proficient to those from the military, but their experience comes from defense, not offense. What they often lack is an understanding of the broad security market, including companies that are anything but cloud-first and cloud-native - Fortune 1000 enterprises, banks, retail and manufacturing businesses, and the like. To succeed, they can partner with people who have some experience working in traditional security teams, and those with a passion for the business side of security.

Another category of founders is security practitioners with experience working on teams at large traditional enterprises or offering services to governments. They are deeply familiar with what it takes to implement security tools in Fortune 500 enterprises and typically have connections at large corporations. What people who spent their careers in security operations centers and service providers lack are experience in building and launching products, and understanding of the needs of cloud-native enterprises, including venture-backed startups. By partnering with practitioners who gained experience at product companies, and those interested in owning the business side of running the startup, they can form a promising team.

Regardless of where founders gained their experience - in the military (typical for Israeli entrepreneurs), at cloud-native product companies (usually based in San Francisco and the Bay Area), or at security teams of large enterprises (often headquartered on the East Coast, particularly in New York or Boston), what matters is that they:

- Have the skills needed to successfully run the company.
- Understand and cater to the needs of traditional, analyst-focused security teams at large enterprises.
- Understand and cater to the needs of modern, engineering-focused security teams at startups and cloud-native product companies.

The reason both customer groups are important is that while startups and cloud-native companies are typically willing to move fast and become design partners, large-scale traditional enterprises are where the money is at. By designing a solution that can be used by both types of customers, startups can iterate quickly with the feedback received from their innovative early adopters, and then move up the market to sell to Fortune 500 and Fortune 1000 enterprises. The security solutions only suitable for cloud-native Bay Area companies suffer from the small market problem. Startups building exclusively for enterprises are often unable to grow because they get stuck in the doom loop: they can't improve their product and iterate fast because they have no active users, and can't get users because sales cycles are incredibly long, and the product is buggy and not ready for the enterprise.

Most cybersecurity entrepreneurs need a co-founder

Having a co-founder is not a must: it is certainly possible to build a security company as a solo founder. The question isn't if it can be done; the question is if taking a certain path is helping, or impeding the probability of a positive outcome. In the early days of a startup, the odds of success are incredibly small and anything founders can do to stack the cards in their favor early is the right thing to do.

Building a startup is a hard and in many ways lonely journey. In the world of information overload, it takes time and a lot of effort to break through the noise, find the right problems to solve, find investors who can best help the company accomplish its mission, and convince industry insiders that they should care about whatever the company is offering. Employees joining early-stage ventures are taking a huge risk, and founders naturally feel responsible for their livelihood. Knowing that the next funding round is never guaranteed and that the company may not get to product-market fit, even when everyone tried hard and did their best, can feel demoralizing.

Having co-founders offers a sounding board, makes it possible to think bigger and broader when looking for ways to solve hard problems, and helps to not destroy the family lives of founders. The latter may sound random, but it isn't. Strong teams can greatly reduce the amount of stress entrepreneurs will be under, and the number of challenges founders end up bringing home to their loved ones. All this is before even considering that the amount of work an early-stage founder needs to do is enormous. It's not just customer discovery and building product, but also sales, fundraising, hiring, marketing & brand building, partnerships, operations, and more. Having several people who can own different areas greatly increases the chances that the startup will succeed.

Seek people who are already doing what you want them to do

Founders spend more time with their co-founders than they do with their partners, and co-founder relationships often outlast many marriages.

If you are going to be spending most of your time in the next decade with a person (or several people), it is important that you don't simply enjoy each other's company, but can also work well together. I find it fascinating how often I'm excited about meeting a smart, well-rounded person, only to find them impossible to work with later. This can happen for many reasons - some people are unwilling to commit, unable to organize their time, have trouble working in teams, get discouraged too easily, and so on.

I think it's critical that before people commit to building a company together, they collaborate on something smaller that allows them to see what working together would feel like. This could be launching an open source project, doing customer discovery and working on a minimum viable product (MVP), or even organizing an event. What's important is going through the motions of brainstorming, planning, executing, and iterating on something together so that they can better understand one another's communication and work style, have transparent discussions about it, and see where the relationship evolves.

I believe that people can best be evaluated by looking at their track record, not by discussing their aspirations. Let me explain what I mean by this.

There are many people out there who are great at talking and painting the most incredible picture of what they could be doing. Although storytelling is a critical skill for a good founder, what matters more in my opinion is their ability to make things happen. By examining what a person has done in the past, it's much easier to think about what they could be capable of in the future.

When I think about a technical co-founder, I think of a person who is already building. They don't need to be building a company, they could be pursuing some passion projects on the side, consistently contributing to open source initiatives (or maybe even launching their own), or at the very least, they are doing something truly incredible as a part of their work. To me personally, side projects are always more convincing because they show that a person is self-driven, motivated & willing to do work without being paid for it. I love seeing people being active in their area of interest - be it security events, Discord channels for practitioners, or their local BSides.

When I think about a business co-founder, I also think of a person who is already doing something about their interests. They could be angel investing or advising startups, organizing events, writing about their areas of interest (product, go-to-market strategies, operations, building companies, etc.), building relationships with security leaders and investors, and so on. They could be pursuing some side projects, looking for ways to make money using no-code and low-code tools, and the like.

Skills are important, but they can be learned; what doesn't change just because a person wants to start a company is the character. In my view, the best co-founders are obsessed with their craft, resourceful to make something out of nothing, and hungry to make things happen when nobody expects they can. I believe that character, values, and beliefs trump hard skills and expertise: those who are driven to learn everything they need to succeed, in a short time can teach themselves a new language, new framework, or new technology.

The easiest way to judge character is to look at small things - how people behave, how they talk, and what excites or frustrates them. Do they show up on time to appointments? If not - what will change when they need to hop on a customer call at 5 am or 10 pm because they are in a different time zone? Are they always late, or do they like to cancel and reschedule their commitments? If so - what will change when a customer is waiting for an answer about their deployment? Do they deliver on their promises? Are they willing to do what it takes to accomplish their goals? Do they get angry when the world doesn't respond the way they expected? Do they have the ability to critically reflect about themselves, their surroundings, and their role in things that happen around them? I have seen founders who take a week to get back to a prospect interested in buying their product, unleash on an employee because they had a bad morning, or don't feel the urgency when a bug is blocking a customer from being able to accomplish a critical task.

As someone who grew up in an orphanage on another side of the planet, moved to Canada in his early twenties without speaking a word of English, and built a career in product despite having no degree from a prestigious school or background in computer science, I always bet on an underdog. I love people who have had something to overcome, something to fight for, something to stand for. I like knowing that a person went through a crucible of some kind - has taken risks, tried something different, challenged the status quo, or pushed themself to do what's uncomfortable. I believe that over the long term, the drive, strong character, resourcefulness, and perseverance will always outperform those who can only work well if they are given all the ingredients they need to be successful.

Expert Insight

"Whether it is selecting a co-founder, or building out the executive leadership team, being as explicit and specific as possible about what your company needs is critical to success. Just because a candidate had fabulous success at another startup in your industry, doesn't mean they are right for your company. For example, are you making a market, or disrupting an existing one? The answer is crucial to knowing what kind of marketing leader you should hire. Making a market requires a high level of creativity, story-telling, domain expertise, PR/AR prowess, etc. A marketer with experience only in disrupting a market someone else has made may struggle. Especially in the early stages, this is true of all business functions - engineering, product management, sales, and marketing; they all must be aligned. The MVP will provide a specific user, with a specific set of circumstances, a specific outcome. Engineering and product management are focused on defining and building an MVP that delivers the outcome. Marketing and sales are focused on finding users with those circumstances and guiding them through a process you can prove results in a sale. In all cases, the leaders and ideally most of their team members will have backgrounds that demonstrate they've done this before and that they are aligned with your business."

- Ted Julian, Co-Founder and CEO at a stealth-mode cybersecurity startup, previously Co-Founder of @stake, Co-Founder of Arbor Networks, and Co-Founder of Resilient

Co-founder dating: being intentional when looking for co-founders

In the US, many entrepreneurs meet their future co-founders at work, which offers a perfect opportunity to see the quality of one another's contributions in action. In Israel, a place for co-founder matching is typically the military, although many cybersecurity founders go back all the way to high school. All of these create natural opportunities to build great friendships that can later lead to starting a company together.

Not everyone, however, is so lucky: some people find themselves in a place where they don't know anyone in their immediate network who would be interested in starting a company together. This can happen for many reasons:

- Potential co-founders could already be working on their own startups.
- The timing might not be right (a prospective co-founder could have just become a parent, got a mortgage, started a lucrative job at a large corporation, etc.).
- The person might not be interested in the cybersecurity industry.

It's also not uncommon to find aspiring founders who haven't been exposed to a large group of people they can pick from. For example, having spent my product career working at small and medium-size startups, I have a more narrow network of former colleagues than someone who has worked as a PM at, say, Google and Microsoft.

One way to meet a prospective co-founder is by going through the so-called co-founder dating - a process of meeting people with the intent of finding someone to build a cybersecurity company with. Co-founder dating is incredibly common in Israel where cybersecurity entrepreneurs attend events, ask for introductions, and conduct informal "reference checks" to see if a person they are talking to could be a solid business partner. In the US, this practice for some reason is less popular, so the overwhelming majority of companies are started by friends or former colleagues. I think it's a big miss: although it makes total sense that people who have worked, studied, or served in the military together could become friends and eventually start exploring what problems are worth solving, co-founder dating can also be a great way to start a company.

Role of VCs in co-founder matching

In mature and rich tech ecosystems such as San Francisco in the US and Tel Aviv in Israel, venture capital firms play a critical role in building companies that extends far beyond their function as capital suppliers. Due to the nature of their work, VCs, especially those focused on early-stage startups, have wide and deep connections in the community. They know who is already experimenting and prototyping early solutions, who is raising capital, who is considering building a company, and who could be a good founder material if they were to find a strong person to partner with.

VCs are connectors - they help startups find partners and early customers, build relationships with potential acquirers, and even find co-founders. Security practitioners interested in starting a company at some point in their lives would greatly benefit from thinking long-term and building relationships with investors in their area of focus. Some of the ways to do it are by offering assistance with due diligence and evaluating tools from the practitioner's point of view, helping to understand trends in the security space, and making introductions to people in their network who are working on early-stage ideas.

Founding teams over duo co-founders

Although it is widely assumed that standard founding teams consist of two people - a technical and a business partner, history has shown that founding teams of three or four people are often the ones that end up building industry-defining companies. From Check Point, Palo Alto Networks, CrowdStrike, Lacework, and Netskope to Snyk, Wiz, and Cloudflare, some of the most influential players in the cybersecurity industry were started by teams of three to four people (Orca Security has 8 co-founders!).

Another assumption is that first-time founders are more likely to form larger founding teams because they would be looking to compensate for the lack of entrepreneurial experience by trying to get more hands on deck. The reality shows something entirely different: many of the entrepreneurs who choose to go for larger founding teams have past experience as founders. Wiz, Palo Alto Networks, CrowdStrike, Snyk, Axonius, and many others have all been built by second, and sometimes third-time founders who, having accumulated a wealth of knowledge of what works best, decided to have larger founding teams. Although based on my observations, Israeli founders are more likely to have large founding teams compared to American entrepreneurs who tend to start companies in duos, experienced founders in the US are beginning to do more of it as well.

I think that having three to four strong co-founders can greatly increase the startup's ability to succeed. Given how many areas need to be covered for the company to move fast (engineering, product, go-to-market, hiring, operations, etc.), having a diverse group of strong founders all pulling in the same direction and leveraging what they can do best can be a tremendous accelerator of growth.

Hiring and managing early employees

Regardless of how big and diverse the founding team is, there comes a time when startups need to hire early employees.

It takes a unique attitude and mindset to be a successful employee at an early-stage company. First and foremost, people must have a sense of urgency and a sense of ownership to move things forward at the speed startups live. Startup founders must hire adults and set expectations clearly: every person needs to have an area they own, an outcome they are trying to drive, a way to know if they are successful, and an ability to expand their area of ownership and take on more. A sense of urgency creates conditions where high performers thrive, and low performers self-select out.

Attracting high performers is not easy and depending on the ecosystem, there may not be an army of people looking to join a high-risk, early-stage venture. If founders are building a company outside of Tel Aviv, the Bay Area, and New York, I think the only way to hire the best is to go fully remote from day one. Startups that originate in one of these three ecosystems may be fortunate to have a somewhat co-located team, at least at the beginning, but that comes at a high cost of talent.

Being a founder means always selling, and recruiting is one of the most critical areas where entrepreneurs get to demonstrate their sales skills. If founders cannot convince people to take a risk and join them on the journey to build a company, chances are they will find it even harder to compel customers to pay for the product they are building.

In an early-stage venture, nobody has enough time to make sure that everyone on the team is going to do the right thing, all the time. This is why founders must focus on establishing the right level of infrastructure, such as communication channels, knowledge base, opportunities for people to contribute ideas outside of their direct area of responsibility, and a way to always be on the same page about the company strategy, direction, and priorities. Additionally, founders should remember that they set the pace and the culture of the early-stage startup, so they should be intentional instead of letting them emerge organically. Simply stating the values is not enough; if entrepreneurs want the right behaviors to take hold, they will have to live what they preach.

Expert Insight

"On the topic of hiring, my suggestion would be to only hire in-network referrals, as long as you possibly can. That's an unpopular opinion because it's slower - possibly dramatically slower, but I think it's better.

If you're able to hire in-network referrals, it's likely to be a better match for both you and the candidate. As much as you believe you know their capabilities, they likely believe they know your capabilities. Your recruiting costs are lower (no recruiting fees) and the anticipated retention is higher, because there is a preexisting relationship established based on mutual trust. Separately, if you can't convince any of the all stars you've previously worked with to come work for you, perhaps there is something wrong with your pitch, mission, vision, or company. It would be good to hear this from people you would expect to otherwise be excited about the opportunity.

When you hire someone you don't know, who isn't a referral from people on the team, there is a lot more pressure on getting the screening of the candidate right. On the other hand, when you hire someone in-network, there is a lot more pressure on getting the pitch right, which is a better task to spend your limited time on. Obviously, if an organization is smaller and suddenly raises $100M in funding, which is expected to be spent in 2 years, hiring only through in-network referrals is a non-starter. But in this case, perhaps the fundraising strategy is wrong, not the hiring one.

Separately, I would argue hiring less people and paying them more is significantly better than hiring more people and paying them less. Almost every employer I've ever observed takes the exact same strategy on hiring, which simply put, involves pressure to hire the best people at the lowest cost and then to retain them, using the least additional dollars possible. Whenever businesses all behave the same way, a question is naturally begged whether an alternative strategy could present itself with disproportionate gains.

If everyone hires as many people as possible, at the prevailing lowest cost, then it means you're deciding to hire more junior people, at a higher volume, which requires more management overhead, which itself is at a higher cost. Why do that? Why hire more junior people and put more pressure on more expensive managers? Why not hire more expensive people, who require less management overhead? The people who get paid more, will work there longer, be retained longer, and present more stability to the business. And having less overall people is easier to manage, producing lower cost at the management layer. Which strategy nets an overall lower cost or an overall faster growth path,

I believe is difficult to quantify. But which strategy results in happier employees who are easier to manage? Definitely the inverse of the norm."

- Anthony Bettini, Founder and CEO at VulnCheck, previously Founder and CEO at FlawCheck and Founder and CEO at Appthority

Deep Dive

To learn what makes some cybersecurity entrepreneurs succeed and others fail, and how various factors impact their ability to compete in the busy market, check out a Venture in Security deep dive titled "On a hunt for successful cybersecurity startups and unicorn founders". You can find it by navigating to https://ventureinsecurity.net/p/on-a-hunt-for-successful-cybersecurity or by scanning this QR code.

Validating the problem

The importance of validating problems in security

I've observed a sentiment in the security community that one needs to experience pain firsthand to identify a problem worth solving. I think this isn't necessarily the case: whether a person experienced the need themselves, or found a problem area by interviewing security leaders and practitioners, in both cases they should be looking to validate the severity of the issue, what types of customers it affects the most, the size of that market, the willingness of buyers to pay for the solution, and the urgency to have the problem solved.

Ideation, customer discovery, and problem validation are especially critical for cybersecurity startups to get right. This is because every organization does security differently, and depending on where one spent their career, they may have drastically different ideas about problems in the industry. A security engineer from a

San Francisco-based, venture-backed high-growth cloud-native startup will think of security differently than a senior analyst from a multi-million retailer headquartered in New York, which is even more different from the perspective of someone who has worked for a managed security services provider that serves hospitals in Texas. Each of their perspectives is equally relevant and equally valid, so the question isn't who is right: it is what problems are worth solving, and which of these solutions are best developed by building a company.

Starting a cybersecurity company without proper validation is akin to moving from a cloud-native startup in Seattle to a bank in Boston, and jumping straight away to implement the tools that worked for the former company, without taking the time to understand the nuances of the new environment, how the business makes money, what its crown jewels are, and what risks it faces.

Thinking about customer segments

One of the most critical questions to answer is who has the problem founders are interested in solving. Too often, I see security entrepreneurs when asked "Who are you solving the problem for?", make broad statements such as "everyone", "large enterprises", and "small and medium businesses (SMBs)". Thinking about the market this way is harmful as it doesn't help focus the development and sales efforts, and ends up pulling the company in many conflicting directions at the same time.

We are used to thinking about picking a target market in security as being a choice between consumer, SMB, and enterprise; in reality, it is much more nuanced. For example:

- A multinational corporation with offices in ten different countries will have different problems than a company serving exclusively the US market.
- A company that is actively buying smaller startups will have unique needs that a business with no M&A strategy wouldn't.
- A cloud-native, 5-year-old technology enterprise with no physical offices will prioritize different problems than a 40-year-old large national retailer with 300+ brick-and-mortar stores.

- A company with 50 employees will have different security needs, depending if it's a tech startup or a small chain of coffee shops.
- A startup that has one IT person and relies on an external service provider to do most of the work is going to see its security needs differently than a startup that has one or two dedicated security people working full-time.
- An enterprise that outsources its security to an externally managed service provider is going to behave differently than one that has a large security team on staff.

To develop a deep understanding of the market, founders need to spend time talking to people from different kinds of organizations. Over time, if they are asking powerful questions and listening intently, they will inevitably start seeing trends.

Find out where different personas are on the technology adoption curve

Companies in any market can be further segmented into different categories based on their attitude toward adopting new technologies. In the book "Crossing the Chasm", Geoffrey Moore talks about the technology adoption lifecycle which begins with innovators and moves to early adopters, early majority, late majority, and laggards. The book discusses a vast chasm that exists between the early adopters and the early majority. While early adopters understand that new technologies have their shortcomings, and are willing to work through bugs and suboptimal experiences, the early majority prefers to wait until everything works smoothly and the new approach has proven its value. This model is highly relevant to cybersecurity where new technologies appear all the time, and buyers behave differently when adopting innovative approaches.

As a part of customer discovery, it is useful to form a hypothesis and map different types of personas to the stage in the technology adoption lifecycle. If it becomes evident that the company is looking to build its business by targeting laggards, it may be wise to look for other segments first that would be willing to act as early adopters.

Thinking about market size and direction

There are two mistakes I commonly see cybersecurity founders make when they are deciding what problems to solve.

The first mistake is picking a target customer without understanding the size of the total addressable market. I often describe this as a security founder's dilemma. People who can build security products mostly come from cloud-native, tech-forward, venture-backed product enterprises that hire security engineers, security architects, and the like. Or, they are ex-intelligence units and agencies, such as Unit 8200 of the Israeli Defense Forces with strong expertise in the offense. In both cases, they are mostly exposed to how security is done in the top 1-5% of most advanced and mature organizations. These tech-forward organizations are also the ones that represent a small percentage of the market and have the resources (i.e., money & talent) to build their own tools. The most painful problems, the biggest opportunities, and the most money to be made are at the traditional, analyst- and compliance-focused companies such as banks, retail firms, oil and gas businesses, and multinational corporations. However, most people who work on their security teams aren't engineers, and it's harder for them to build solutions to their organization's problems. This gets worse when we look at small and medium businesses: they rarely hire deeply technical security talent, so practitioners who could be building impactful solutions never get to learn about the problems SMBs experience. Hence the dilemma: while security practitioners from cloud-native companies in the US and IDF in Israel tackle cutting-edge problems and think about the promising future, the less futuristic, mundane problems experienced by the mass market continue to persist. Too many startups that are being built today are fighting to solve problems of the top 3-5% of the market, only to realize that they will quickly outgrow their market and hit a plateau.

The second mistake is overestimating the speed with which the market is changing in the short-term, and underestimating it in the long-term. We have seen this with the adoption of the cloud, and we are seeing it now with AI. Understanding the speed of market evolution and the nuances surrounding it is critical to building a successful startup and making bets that are more likely to pay off. For example, although it is clear that the percentage of companies exclusively relying on the on-prem infrastructure is shrinking, founders have to be realistic about the speed of growth of cloud-native enterprises we will see in the next several years.

Gauging urgency and the willingness to pay

Every company is dealing with thousands of problems, and although all of them deserve to be solved, founders need to pick their battles wisely, especially if they are looking to build a company, not just a product.

Enterprises tackle their security needs as projects, so what area the company is going to focus on, and when it is going to be worked upon, are defined several quarters in advance. This means that unlike what some founders would want to believe, an enterprise isn't likely to do a proof of value (POV) of their tool after they see a demo unless it aligns with their priorities for the upcoming quarter or two.

The lack of urgency on the customer side to solve the problems the startup is exploring immediately does not mean that the idea isn't worth pursuing. If there are trends and underlying reasons why it will become a pressing issue in a year or two, then building the solution may still be worth it. However, founders need to validate their assumptions and make sure that they are not being blindsided by their excitement about solving the problem. In most cases, unless it is really deep tech with a high chance of meeting an emerging market need (think of security for quantum computing), taking this path is incredibly risky, and in most cases, not worth it.

Looking for problems worth solving

When you are passionate about tackling an important problem, you don't necessarily need to worry about starting a business. Some problems are best solved as open source projects, online courses, or even an article outlining steps someone else can take to improve their organization's security posture. However, if you are looking to launch a startup, you will need to pick a problem worth solving.

There are no set criteria of how that should look like; here are some thoughts to consider as you are working on ideation:

- All problems can be divided into two buckets - vitamins and painkillers. Vitamins are nice to have, so people don't feel urgency to buy them and when budgets get cut, they are the first to go. Painkillers are essential as they solve hard problems. As much as possible, founders should be looking to build painkillers, not vitamins.
- Some problems are too nebulous and generic; I call these "boiling the ocean" problems. They are impactful and important to solve; the challenge is that solving them requires an ecosystem player. For example, hundreds of people would like to change the way security products are bought but as long as the current model works for sellers and buyers, it's unlikely a small startup can shift how thousands of parties collaborate. It's akin to replacing the DNS protocol: theoretically it can be done, but there are so many players interested in preserving the system they rely on today that it may not be the right problem to tackle, especially for a first-time founder.
- Some problems call for novel approaches, while others can be solved by iterating on the existing solutions. Both can be worth doing as long as founders understand the trade-offs. Establishing a new market category calls for founders who are willing to spend a lot of time educating the industry. If there is no appetite for this work, entrepreneurs are better off focusing on building a 2.0 version of an existing solution.
- Some problems extend beyond security even if they are especially painful in security operations. I am quite interested in these as they have much bigger markets than cybersecurity tooling. For example, security orchestration and automation is just one use case of the broader enterprise automation problem, hence companies that start as a SOC automation platform can later expand beyond security.
- Some problem areas bypass the need to go directly to CISOs or create an opportunity to cross-sell to other personas within the enterprise. Depending on the way security teams are

structured, identity security, identity verification, anti-fraud, and data security solutions may be good examples of these.

It is important to not only understand the technical side of the problem but also the broader context surrounding it, including affected parties and incentives that impact their decisions. If the solution you are proposing makes someone's life harder or makes them lose political capital in their organization, you are likely to see a lot of resistance.

Conducting problem and idea discovery: a tactical approach

As a part of the ideation process, you will need to become an expert in your area of interest. This involves a lot of reading, research, and forming early hypotheses, as well as talking to people who play an active role in the security ecosystem such as analysts, resellers, integrators, and service providers. After you have shortlisted problem areas you would like to explore, it's time to reach out to two categories of people you should care about the most: users and buyers of security solutions.

The users of security tools are typically cybersecurity and compliance practitioners - security analysts, security engineers, SOC architects, detection engineers, penetration testers, compliance managers, IT administrators, and the like. Although security practitioners do not particularly enjoy talking to vendors about the tools they use at work, they are more than willing to discuss industry problems, especially when attending events and conferences such as BSides, Blue Team Con, and the ACoD - Art into Science conference. Going where security practitioners congregate, online and offline, and asking open-ended questions is a great way to learn.

The economic buyers of security tools are Chief Information Security Officers and sometimes their deputies, vice presidents, or directors, one or two levels below CISO. Because there are more vendors than there are CISOs of large enterprises, each security leader is bombarded with hundreds of emails and demo requests weekly. I don't have the perfect advice for reaching CISOs other than working through your network, former colleagues, VCs, and angel investors, and asking for help. Attending CISO-focused events can also work, but you will need to be very upfront with security leaders that you aren't there to pitch. This isn't easy because many founders have broken trust with their aggressive sales tactics. Once you get to the CISO that likes what you are doing, ask them for a connection to three peers who might want to talk about the problem space. Three is a good number - one might not answer, and a second one might be too busy, so having three introductions greatly increases the chances of success.

As you do the customer discovery calls, different frameworks and approaches can help you structure the process and not get lost in the multitude of ideas and perspectives. I recommend diving into the problem areas, synthesizing learnings, and then shortlisting all the ideas to two or three that appear most promising. To narrow the list down to one idea, reach out to a pool of 10-25 CISOs and practitioners and learn as much as you can about the problem, what they've tried, what they are currently using to solve it, etc. When you are down to one problem you want to pursue, talk to as many CISOs and practitioners as you can (at least 40 or 50) to go as deep as humanly possible and validate the problem area further. Every interview will lead to more learnings, better-refined hypotheses, better-phrased questions, and new connections with security professionals who feel the pain you are looking to address daily.

Outcomes of problem and idea discovery

At the end of the ideation and problem discovery, you should have narrowed down a problem area to focus on and have good answers to a wide variety of questions including:

- The scope and impact of the problem.
- Types of customers who experience it and the ideal customer profile.
- The solutions people rely on today and why they fall short of their expectations.
- What an ideal solution and a minimum viable product looks like.

- Why no one has solved this problem until now and whether the solution is feasible.
- What the buying journey looks like for the product, who is involved, and in what way.
- What the expected budget for the solution is.
- The risks and challenges that can kill your company if you were to pursue this idea.
- The characteristics of early adopters in the segment (ideally, accompanied by a list of people who are excited about what you are working on and interested in becoming design partners).
- Whether this problem is worth solving, and if it is, if you are well-positioned to work on the solution.
- Questions the answers to which you do not yet know, assumptions you are making, and areas that you will need clarity on as you go.

The goal isn't to get stuck in a permanent discovery process but to accumulate as much learning as possible as quickly as possible before going ahead to build a solution. There is little worse for an early-stage startup than jumping into problem-solving without understanding different facets of the problem, the degree to which it is preventing people from accomplishing their goals, and the size of the market (the number of organizations affected by the problem).

Asking questions the right way

Time and time again I see founders get on the call to do what they think is customer discovery only to pitch their solution, and a few minutes before the conversation is scheduled to end, ask "So what do you think?". Although it is incredibly common, this approach does not lead to valuable learning. Most people want to be helpful and uplifting, and because they know that building a startup is hard, they want to encourage founders to keep going so they say things like "This sounds like a good idea" and "I would definitely try it".

To get the information founders need, they must first and foremost change their way of asking questions. This means, among other things:

- Not pitching your solution. No matter how great you think your perspectives and ideas are, the goal of discovery interviews is to listen and learn.
- Replacing hypothetical questions and questions about the future with questions about specific behaviors people have exhibited in the past. Instead of asking "Would you use X?", say "Walk me through the time when you ran into this problem in the past - how did you go about solving it?". People don't know what the future looks like so answers to questions such as "Would you pay $10 for this new generation password manager?" do not provide anything of value.
- Replacing closed-ended, confirmation-style questions with open-ended inquiries rooted in curiosity. For example, instead of asking "Do you like your current tool X?", say "Tell me about your experience using X to solve the problem?".
- Focusing on different facets of the experience. Few things are completely good or completely bad; most have a bit of both. To build a more comprehensive picture, you may ask "What works well about it, and what is hard? What makes it hard?".
- Avoid always asking "why" because it can sometimes put people in a defensive mode. It can be helpful to replace "why" with "what" or "how", i.e., changing "Why is it hard?" to "What makes it hard?".

As humans, once we are engaged in the conversation, we tend to forget about best practices and launch into our default pitching mode. To avoid doing it, it's helpful to prepare a list of questions you are looking to ask ahead of time - not to be rigid but to focus the conversation around what matters and to keep yourself from slipping into pitching.

Lastly, don't forget to take good notes. Most security leaders and practitioners won't be comfortable sharing sensitive data on the call that is being recorded, so it's a good idea to get a co-founder to take notes. Note-taking is important because we tend to only remember highlights, and things people said that resonated with us, and discard what goes against our beliefs even if it is equally (or more) useful. Having several founders process the same information is likely to lead to a productive debrief and brainstorming afterward.

For people looking to get better at asking powerful questions, I highly recommend "The Mom Test" by Rob Fitzpatrick. It's a short, easy-to-digest, and very practical book that offers a great set of practices for effective customer and problem discovery. This book will teach you how to stop asking questions such as "Would you like to have the ability to do X?" (most people will say "yes"), or "Would you use X if we built it?" (most people will say "yes" as well). Instead, it will help you frame questions to learn what people actually think and do. For example, "Explain your workflow to me. What is hard about it? What problems did you run into? How did you try to solve these problems when you ran into them last time? What worked, and what didn't?".

Expert Insight

"We, cybersecurity founders, are often cyber-problem focused. However, we must extend our understanding to the business side of the problem. First, we need to understand the business value that is created if the problem is solved. Second, we must understand the organizational and business reasons which are the cornerstone of the problem. Validating if the problem creates real friction between the business and the security is important to find problems worth solving."

- Idan Gour, Co-Founder and CTO at Astrix Security

Expert Insight

"The 2020s ushered in the pervasive echo chamber effect in news and social media, numbing our alertness to confirmation bias. In the cybersecurity domain, this effect is particularly pronounced. The industry's vulnerability to this

phenomenon stems from homogenous backgrounds and close-knit networking circles, often amplified by trend-setters like industry analyst firms and VC-backed CISO networks. Furthermore, security teams and CISOs open to experimenting with emerging technologies from startups are typically tech-forward and early adopters, which further skews critical thinking.

To counter this, founders must practice 'decision hygiene' (as Daniel Kahneman calls it in his book 'Noise') to avoid falling in love with a problem that seems prevalent but is actually limited in scope. A deliberate effort to integrate a diverse array of perspectives (have you considered grabbing coffee with a corporate PM? They probably have a thesis on your problem, and no, they won't steal your idea), and establishing checkpoints for unbiased feedback are crucial. These steps ensure the problem being tackled is not just a buzz in a closed-circle group but a widespread, genuine pain point with robust market potential."

- Dor Morgenstern, Senior Product Manager at Torq
and Founder of the Founders Circle at 8200 Young Forum

Expert Insight

"When it comes to engaging with security practitioners about problem validation, the right context, and framing can make all the difference.

The dynamic between vendors and practitioners has long been strained, often due to a history of unmet expectations, growth at all costs, and unfulfilled promises. Those ghosts continue to haunt the present day and are the undercurrent of the relationships between the two sides. In a high-stakes world like cybersecurity where every choice carries weight, misalignments are more than just setbacks, they are outright roadblocks.

True progress in cybersecurity transcends making sales and getting new logos. It's about fundamentally aligning and elevating the needs of practitioners, enabling them to do tomorrow what they cannot do today. To make that kind of impact, you have to start with trust and prove it time and again. It's a challenging journey, regardless of which side you're on, but when navigated skillfully, it paves the way for genuine industry advancement."

- Mike Privette, independent industry analyst writing at Return On Security, advisor, and angel investor

Building cybersecurity products

Pivot away from traditional product management frameworks

The role of a founder is to be an expert in the problem space. This fact stays the same regardless of what industry they are in, and whether they are building a consumer app, conceiving the next-generation cybersecurity tool, or trying to change the way agriculture works.

While product management as a discipline does not change depending on the industry, cybersecurity is without a doubt a space that does not accept templated approaches.

A lot of what is known as product management best practices comes from the hyper-growth experiences of consumer-focused Silicon Valley companies such as Meta, Google, Instagram, and Netflix. The idea is that founders and product leaders can subsidize user growth, leverage referrals, growth loops, and virality to scale the number of daily active users (DAU) quickly, and only then think about figuring out the monetization. Tools like feature flagging, A/B testing, cohort analysis, regressions, and others along with different ways to engage users such as gamification were created precisely in the B2C space. It is much harder to leverage these approaches when building cybersecurity products. There are several reasons why that is the case:

- The install base is substantially lower as few cybersecurity products get mass adoption and the vast majority are B2B.
- The vast majority of what we think of as cybersecurity is based on enterprise sales with long product evaluations, slow adoption cycles, and a heavy reliance on trust and personal relationships for purchasing.
- Founders and product leaders in security are building the product for expert users who often know the domain much better than vendors.
- Short release cycles that work well for select cloud-native companies built in the cloud and for the cloud, do not work for the majority of the vendors forced to support obscure technologies, legacy architecture, and on-prem solutions.
- Security needs are heavily defined by the companies' unique processes, operations, tech stack, geography, and a myriad of other factors which makes it hard to come up with a one-size-fits-all solution.

Instead of providing founders with the ability to iterate quickly and often, and introduce impactful user experience enhancements, cybersecurity presents a complex puzzle with a large number of conflicting inputs to consider. A proof of value (POV) can take months before the product team learns what worked and what didn't. Many factors that influence buying decisions are completely outside of the founders' and product leaders' control (such as meeting various compliance requirements, and satisfying frameworks and standards).

The importance of the trust factor is so high that any small perceived gap discovered during the POV can jeopardize the potential partnership. While having a green checkbox icon with a lock and the words "Secure and PCI compliant" may be enough for a consumer app to reduce the fear of customers putting in their credit card details, much more is needed to convince a large enterprise to deploy a tool from an unknown startup on their network.

To put it simply, the modern product management theory and best practices do not prepare founders for the level of complexity that is a norm in cybersecurity. Although there are no easy ways to deal with this problem, I have found the following to be a useful mental model for thinking about solutions:

- Start with your ideal customer profile and build a deep understanding of their needs, pain points, use cases they want to see addressed, and their ability to influence the buying process.
- Assume that many of the so-called "best practices", especially those that come from the B2C space, are either not going to work or will have a different shape when implemented in security (this applies to growth loops and product-led growth).
- Adopt an evidence-based approach that enables you to test and validate your hypothesis and find what works best for your product.

Expert Insight

"Having had the good fortune of discovering my passion and working in the cybersecurity industry for the past decade and a half, and while my journey started as a security consultant turned innovation strategist, I quickly realized that I could create a much higher impact by building transformative cybersecurity products. During this time, I played a myriad of roles in and around security products - user, independent evaluator, alliance partner, customer, product manager, product marketer, and even a seller.

The sheer amount of breach news, regulation, and high valuation commanded by security companies in both private and public markets has created an explosion of security products, often causing confusion and chaos in the minds of the customer due to overlapping features and unclear messaging. In my opinion, this has happened partly because the market recently got flooded with builders who have limited to no understanding of the customers' pain points, and who were hoping to capitalize on the cybersecurity hype. Many security leaders started their own companies thinking that since they dealt with the problem firsthand, they can easily build and sell a product that everyone wants.

To maximize the value of your time spent reading this, here are my top 5 tips on building security products for enterprise customers at scale:

Boring problems have a larger market. *You may have created a unique solution with the help of your large engineering squad at your big tech co, but you will soon come to see that your solution's pre-requisite/smarts are not a fit for most customers you approach. Find the painful problems that unlock value for most if not all enterprises. Vanta is one of my favorite examples for this one as they expanded their addressable market by focusing on the most boring yet essential parts of the compliance problem.*

Get obsessed about the problem. *Product managers have a double-edged sword of bias to action i.e. they are raring to ship a product. While perfect is the enemy of good, if your vision is flawed, nothing you build will look right. Wait until you have a deep understanding of the problem to formulate an effective vision. Wiz has executed this vision of entering a fairly crowded market of cloud security and creating high impact with a product that solves the most painful problem of minimizing remediation time with maximum impact.*

Be data-driven but focus on simplicity and usability. *Remember that most security teams are tight on time and budget, so the last thing they need is something you made optimizing highly on data but low on user empathy and intuition. Gone are the days when users would get a certification to use your product, so try and make it easy enough so that a fresh college grad can create value and solve their problems with your solution.*

Don't hurry into becoming a platform. *While this may seem like a simple market expansion question, you lose your core value the minute you start creating a suite of products. While bear markets bring consolidation and platforms* *are easier to buy, best-of-breed specialized products will always be preferred long-term by savvy buyers provided you get the rest of them right. Unsure what the future will bring for Snyk, but 2023 isn't going well for them due to this hurried amalgamation of products they platformed together.*

Play nicely with the ecosystem. *Your walled garden is neither useful nor easy to use. In the age of microservices and APIs, if you don't unlock data portability with your product, you will likely be replaced with a competitor that supports more integrations. Early focus on integrations to both ingest and send data to enable workflows are going to be considered differentiated in a crowded market. As for those of you who belong to the old school of "my product, my data, precious", you will do well to remember that we live in the age of co-opetition and customers will likely have overlapping products to minimize concentration risks. Splunk did this really well, partly because they had to due to the nature of their product, but they ended up creating a solid solution to ingesting every single security data type and source.*

Lastly, remember to stay in close touch with your go-to-market teams. In cybersecurity, there's an old saying - 'Customers are more likely to buy the best marketed product than the best made one', i.e. you have to balance the smarts of your product with relevant messaging and timing. Your sales and marketing teams will make or break your product's viability, so make them your best friends. CrowdStrike is my favorite example of balancing product development with visionary and powerful go-to-market execution."

- Nipun Gupta, Chief Operating Officer at Bearer, startup advisor, and angel investor

Look for ways to overcome challenges of customer discovery

In most industries, buyers and end users are happy to talk to vendors because they recognize that software providers are there to identify their problems, pain points, and inefficiencies, and build solutions that remove them. The same, unfortunately, cannot be said about cybersecurity where few leaders or practitioners are open to having transparent conversations with strangers. There are several reasons why this is the case. First, security teams are chronically overextended and understaffed, and therefore cannot prioritize talking to founders over improving the security posture of their companies. Second, CISOs and practitioners alike are inundated by vendors who reach out to them from all fronts - calls, emails, social media messages, and conferences, to name a few. Lastly, founders and adversaries are looking for answers to the same kinds of questions - what products the company is using, which of them are failing, and where the coverage gaps are. Needless to say, without a strong level of trust between the parties, most security teams would not be comfortable providing the answers to a stranger. All this makes the lives of cybersecurity entrepreneurs and product leaders incredibly hard.

There are several ways to overcome the challenges of customer discovery.

Talking to customers is important but it's not the only way to become an expert on the problem space. I found that many people in security are much more open to sharing their feedback in a survey or via email rather than in a video call. Although it will never provide as much context as a conversation, in the absence of alternatives it is a good start.

Most cybersecurity startups do not have thousands or even hundreds of paying customers to talk to. And, when founders and product managers reach out to people in the industry who are not yet customers, they find that most security professionals don't want to share their problems with strangers. One way to overcome this limitation is to build trust through events and community initiatives. Attending conferences can be a great way to talk to people who are not currently using your tool; not to sell, but to learn how to solve their problems and build better products. I have personally found smaller conferences for practitioners like BSides and Blue Team Con to be great places for problem-discovery conversations. People at these events are generally quite open to chatting, especially if you make it fun, not sales-oriented, and if you approach them without any hidden agenda. Most practitioners are very receptive and happy to help when they see someone show genuine interest in their work instead of trying to sell them some magic next-gen security tool.

Do not over-optimize technology and under-optimize the business model

Because cybersecurity requires deep domain expertise, the vast majority of the founders and product leaders tend to have a technical background. This, combined with the objective of ensuring that technology is well designed, optimized, and works as intended, tends to make them put a lot of effort into building a good product. And, since the time entrepreneurs have to tackle problems is finite, and conflicting priorities make it hard to do everything at once, the business side of the product tends to suffer.

In practical terms, this means that frequently, the business model the company is trying to pursue is not viable from day one, the unit economics don't leave any room for profitable margins, or the support costs are going to scale with the company reducing the customer lifetime value (CLV). Understanding the underlying economics of building a product can help founders avoid costly mistakes.

Here are some of the ways to address this:

- Before building the product, do the modeling in a simple Excel spreadsheet to understand what needs to be true for metrics such as customer acquisition costs (CAC), customer lifetime value (CLV), average order size, cost of goods sold (COGS), and gross margin (GM), to name a few, to make financial sense. If you are not familiar with these terms, you should most definitely prioritize learning them early on your journey.

- Identify scenarios in which the actual performance under these metrics puts the business model of the company under question.
- State assumptions as to what each of these numbers will look like when the product is launched and is being actively used by the customers.
- Compare the actual metrics against the projections to validate (or invalidate) assumptions, identify red flags early, and further optimize the business model.

Avoid thinking about the buying journey in simplistic terms

It is common, especially for first-time founders, to oversimplify the buying journey for their product. Some startups think "We just need to convince a CISO that we are better than alternative options" while others go another route and talk about "Just doing product-led growth and going bottom-up". Unfortunately for both, neither is how security products are actually purchased. The mechanics will heavily depend on the specific product and a market segment, but it is common for hands-on practitioners, CISOs, compliance, legal, finance, and purchasing departments to evaluate new tools from their unique lenses. For some products, the list may also include chief technology officers (CTOs), software developers, and engineering managers. Different parties will have different roles and different levels of influence on the final decision depending on the organization's size, structure, power dynamics, and other factors. Furthermore, as a part of making the buying decision, the prospect's security team will interrogate the vendor's own security posture. This is a very uncommon loop as, for example, no company buying accounting software will be given the chance to review the vendor's accounting practices.

Although there are no easy ways to reduce the complexity surrounding the buying journey, I have found that the number one step is to identify who is involved in the purchasing process, what they care about, what their influence is, what angles they are looking at the problem from, and capture it in a visual artifact. This will make it significantly easier to have a conversation and to understand what your product and the company need to offer to each party to satisfy their requirements. Keep in mind the incentives that drive the decision-making of different parties will vary widely. To shorten the sales cycle and increase the chances of converting the customer, you will want to ensure that your product is not introducing friction or upsetting anyone who has the chance to impact its adoption.

Navigate the custom ways in which every organization does security

Every organization's environment is different, and therefore every company does security in its own way. This means that workflows, playbooks, risks, attack vectors, and what constitutes a "suitable security coverage" will vary greatly from one company to another. This complexity and variability make the lives of product leaders quite hard: every customer they talk to will inevitably bring their must-have feature requests. Dealing with this can be overwhelming, especially because from the outside, many of these organizations with unique needs will fall under the same customer profile.

Building everything users ask for is not possible: not only would it result in Frankenstein products, but also no company has enough resources to do that. On the other hand, not responding to the needs customers are being vocal about can result in issues with adoption, or high churn rates. To address this dilemma,

- Companies should look for ways to design their products as building blocks and make them extendable by using open APIs and the latest technical design principles.
- Founders must understand the willingness and the ability of the customers in a particular segment to tailor out-of-the-box products to their needs.
- Product leaders should conduct thorough customer research to understand what the 80% of product functionality needed by all customers is, and what the remaining 20% is that users can do on their own (this assumes that there are self-serve ways for them to extend the functionality of the product).

Expert Insight

"Exceptional reporting makes a product stand out, and shows you understand your customer's operating reality. What matters to your product's engineering or analyst user base is going to be different than what matters to their CISO – make sure you address both. Technical teams often struggle to translate their work efforts into reports that speak to business impacts. Giving the engineers an easy way to report the business outcomes of your product – time saved, performance against peer averages, even measurable coverage improvements – will have your users wondering what they were doing before they started using your solution."

- Paul Caiazzo, Chief Growth Officer at SnapAttack

Pick the core focus early

Some problems are only seen in one market segment, while others span several types of customers at once. For those that are common across both consumer, SMB, and enterprise space, a startup would usually look to penetrate one of the segments first, and then seek adoption across others. Think about productivity tools as an example: individuals, small businesses, and large corporations all need to manage tasks and projects. While the scale and some nuances do vary, we often see that what distinguishes a consumer-focused task manager from an enterprise-focused one are multi-tenancy and multi-user support, role-based access control (RBAC), API access, single sign-on (SSO), and access to audit logs.

Although individuals, Fortune 1000 companies, and everyone in between needs cybersecurity, what they see as "security" varies. Individuals are notorious for not wanting to adopt (not to mention having to pay for) anything that introduces friction. Small and medium-sized businesses are only now starting to realize that they do need security; for them, security means having an "everything-in-one solution". Enterprises, on the other hand, require advanced capabilities that are API-first, and much more specialized than SMB-focused tools. A security product that started by targeting consumers cannot typically move up the market, and vice versa. An enterprise solution for network detection and response (NDR), for example, cannot be simplified to the consumer level because consumers don't need or care about network security. A personal identity and a credit history monitoring solution, on the other hand, offers little room to be extended into an enterprise product.

To address this reality, founders and product leaders need to understand their target market, and the kind of solutions they are looking for. Furthermore, startups should commit to solving a problem for a well-defined subset of the market while realizing that with few exceptions, they cannot hope for cross-customer segment mobility. B2C solutions will remain B2C-focused, enterprise-centric tools will struggle to sell to SMBs, etc.

Be careful when listening to power users

When you build an enterprise-focused security product, you are working with experts who have well-formed strong opinions, and who will immediately say what they do and don't care about. This is a blessing and a curse of cybersecurity because every person comes with their ideas, and in the context of their organization, the perspective they bring is likely correct. Each organization's environment is different, and each company's workflows are unique, so what works for one customer may not work for another. Each has a legitimate need to do things their way and the product they buy needs to offer a path for different implementations.

Security is one of the few industries where the end user is more knowledgeable about the subject matter than the vendor. For comparison, few Netflix users are experts in movie creation and machine learning algorithms. Even in IT, companies are selling to technical buyers whose expertise is typically broad but somewhat shallow (they know a little about a lot), while the vendor's expertise is narrow but deep in their respective area (say, storage).

When security professionals get very loud about their needs, they can often pressure product teams into building functionality unique to their setup and not useful for other customers. This is especially the case with power users who tend to be more proactive, vocal, descriptive, and offer actionable ideas. Founders get excited when talking to these power users as they are the ones who "get it", and it always feels great to get the feedback that product teams can act upon immediately, from someone who is using the tool the way founders envisioned it. The challenge is that power users typically represent a small percentage of the customer base, and building products on their feedback alone will inevitably add more complexity, which in turn can alienate others who aren't as technologically proficient. By optimizing exclusively for the needs of power users, the company can diverge from its target market, the problems of which may be different than those of the top 1-5% of the most advanced customers.

Build scalable systems to aggregate customer feedback

Customers share their feedback all around - in sales demos, in Slack, over email, and in conversations with support. Unless aggregated in one place, triaged, and organized, all this is just a cacophony of ideas and perspectives. Many great tools help make sense of customer feedback. Whichever solution you choose (tools are just that, tools), what matters is the ability to group the notes, see trends over time, spot patterns, and use these insights to prioritize product development and go-to-market efforts.

Too often, triaging customer feedback is left to technical co-founders. I think doing this is a mistake. While they are mining for gold, they are not the only people in the company doing that. Those in charge of sales, customer support, sales engineering, and marketing, be they the co-founders or employees, all talk to customers and learn what is important to them. The challenge is that quite often, these golden nuggets of insights and feedback do not make it back to founders who can aggregate, organize, and use them as input in prioritization and planning the go-to-market strategy, not just for building new features.

Early-stage founders should look for ways to establish lightweight systems and processes that encourage everyone in the company to share their discoveries and have them captured in a central repository. To get started, they can include a question about customer feedback ("What are people telling you? What have you learned?") in their regular one-on-one with everyone in the company. It doesn't have to be done formally, especially at an early-stage startup when the team is still small.

Although systems are important, the hardest part for most founders, from what I have seen, is not setting up tools that aggregate notes from customer calls, but embracing a beginner's mindset and being truly open to hearing what customers have to say. Because security requires deep technical expertise, most entrepreneurs in the space come from the industry after having accumulated many years of work experience. A big part of building a product is embracing that they don't have all the answers, and approaching the problem from a curiosity standpoint. This can be hard for some security professionals who have previously achieved growth precisely because of their ability to predict, anticipate, and have the answers. Founders with an ambition to build successful companies need to embrace the beginner's mindset and learn to listen with curiosity.

Keep in mind that today's products are tomorrow's features

In cybersecurity, today's products are tomorrow's features. When a new concept, a new technology, or a new threat vector emerges, startups are usually quick to build a stand-alone product that addresses the problem. They move fast and get some traction with it, often enough to get acquired or expand a small feature into a broader solution. Over time, however, as the new concept becomes accepted and well-understood, yesterday's product becomes a feature of a larger platform and it's no longer possible to use it as a way to enter the market.

Expert Insight

"Sometimes there isn't an existing security product that quite fits your organization's needs. What do you do? Many 'modern' security teams have moved from a focus on 'breaking' (find all the vulnerabilities) to 'building', asking

themselves: 'What are the tools, libraries, and infrastructure we can build that can help our developer colleagues ship software quickly and securely?'.

As many modern security teams focus on hiring security professionals who can also code (or even hire software engineers outright), they can build internally what doesn't yet exist on the market.

Oftentimes, that same risk or security pain point one company experiences is shared by many companies. So the people who build the original version for their company end up leaving to found a startup to productize the idea and sell that same solution to many customers. This has happened many times and will be a continuing trend, but to name a few examples:

After building and releasing ConsoleMe, a just-in-time access control system for Netflix, ***Curtis Castrapel founded Noq Software****.*

After wanting a cloud-native, highly scalable tool for modern detection and response engineers, ***Jack Naglieri built and open sourced StreamAlert at Airbnb before founding Panther****.*

After investing in creating secure-by-default infrastructure building blocks at Netflix, ***Travis McPeak and Aladdin Almubayed founded Resourcely****.*

Ask yourself: 'What important security pain points does my company have?'. Then build a solution while getting paid by your day job, and learn about all the edge cases and tough architecture choices. Talk to a few friends at other companies to see if they also have the same problem. If so, you're in a good position to leave your job to found a company building a product that solves the same pain point. Bonus points: give conference talks about what you've built while you're still at your day job to increase your personal brand and reputation in this area, and open source what you've built to gauge people's interest, and so you don't have to start from scratch when you found a company."

- Clint Gibler, the creator of tl;dr sec, a free weekly newsletter read by over 30,000 cybersecurity practitioners to CISOs, founders, and VCs

Navigating funding options

Making sense of the fundraising complexity

Given the complexity of fundraising, including different types of investors, different ways in which they evaluate companies and allocate capital, and the fact that many VCs heavily rely on personal relationships and warm introductions, it is no wonder that an average founder gets overwhelmed by fundraising.

Despite the complexity, I strongly believe that founders need to understand the options they have access to, and the nuances surrounding each of them. While solving hard problems for companies willing to pay for having them solved is more important than fundraising, bad fundraising decisions can have a negative impact on the future of the company. In this section, I will share some of the thoughts and perspectives surrounding the topic of growth capital. None of this is by any means "right" or universally applicable, but I think it may be useful for entrepreneurs new to the topic of fundraising.

Focus on solving the problem & growing business, not raising capital

Good founders should focus first and foremost on building sustainable, long-term businesses that generate immense value, not on raising capital. There is a persistent imbalance in any economy; great companies will see an oversupply of capital and investors interested in writing them a check, while most startups will struggle chasing funding and getting denied every step of the way. Knowing that this is the case, entrepreneurs will be better off working to build great companies.

There is now a whole army of social media influencers and consultants focused on helping founders get better-looking slides.

Instead of spending precious time listening to their advice, I think that founders should always go back to first principles and ask themselves what investors care about, what their interests are, and what they are incentivized to do. Neither VCs nor angels are in the business of evaluating graphics and designs. VCs are looking for great teams capable of executing well, large markets, and opportunities to make money for their Limited Partners. Angels are seeking teams tackling problems they can get behind, or companies that will be looking to grow fast and mark up the paper valuation quickly so that they can sell their stake to VCs in a few short years. The pitch deck should look presentable but getting the graphics perfect is not time well spent. Instead, founders should be signing up more design partners, getting more customers to say "yes", and doing what it takes to make the revenue numbers go up.

It is worth mentioning that not everyone should be looking to raise capital - some companies can certainly be bootstrapped. The challenge is that many security startups require significant upfront investment for research and development, building proprietary threat intelligence capabilities, or purchasing expensive computing infrastructure. For example, it would not be possible to invest in the infrastructure required to establish a leading cloud provider by bootstrapping. At the same time, it should be possible to grow a small services or a product company to $1-$10 million in annual recurring revenue, if this meets the goals of the founders. Bootstrapping offers a way to build a business without having to deal with a form of external management (boards, investors, etc.), and do it while being grounded in the reality of the market. Most importantly, it can save founders a huge amount of dilution on the cap table: if they are bootstrapped, and invest that into R&D, they will have much stronger unit economics for when (and if) they do choose to fundraise.

Get the angels from your network on board

Most startups are better off validating the problem space, their solution, and the market before they approach VCs to raise capital. There are many reasons why founders should be looking to get their first check from the angels:

- Raising money from angels is much easier and faster. There is no need to involve lawyers, negotiate a valuation, or attend dozens of meetings with different people as a part of due diligence.
- Angels are often highly engaged and ready to help to get the company off the ground. CISOs could make introductions to their peers, security analysts and engineers can help test the product, and experienced operators can support founders by sharing expertise in their area (product, marketing, sales, etc.). Regardless of the individual backgrounds, every angel can add value to the company in ways that most VCs don't have the capacity for.
- Having several credible angels on board will make raising money from VCs easier. VCs are looking for signals, and seeing reputable people who believe in the company's success can help VCs develop conviction quickly. Moreover, angels are super-connectors, and many are happy to make warm introductions to VCs when the time is right.

At the earliest stages when there is just an idea, a basic prototype, or a beta version of the product, startups don't need that much capital. What they need is an ability to maintain focus on the opportunity, just enough money to cover the basics, and a more or less impartial party to point out the blind spots and help course-correct if the team gets off track. Negotiating a valuation at such an early stage would be an unnecessary distraction.

I discussed the value-add of angels, angel syndicates, and angel networks in-depth earlier in the book. For founders or aspiring entrepreneurs looking for resources to understand how to pitch and work with angels, I highly recommend the book "Angel" by Jason Calacanis.

Working with VCs

The best way to build relationships with VCs is to do it before you need them - a rule that applies to human relationships in general. Offering your help in evaluating potential investments, advising or otherwise supporting their portfolio companies, and being active in the industry more broadly are some of the ways to do it.

Many entrepreneurs dislike the fact that VCs heavily rely on warm introductions. I am a big believer in accepting the reality as is and playing with the cards we are dealt. Venture capital firms are always on the lookout for new ideas and promising founders, so simply updating the LinkedIn page to say "Founder in Stealth" will get you solid inbound interest. Having said that, I think it's smart to be proactive and connect with investors you would like to get funded by. One of the easiest ways to get the right warm introduction is to reach out to the founders from VC's current portfolio companies. This has several benefits. First, entrepreneurs are always happy to help others stepping on a similar path, and will often gladly take a 20-minute call. After that they would have learned enough to make an introduction to their VC if it makes sense and for both parties to connect. Second, I think founders should be doing the background check of the VCs they consider working with; a good place to start is to learn about their style, values, and what they care about before pitching. There is no better way to learn about working with a VC than to ask founders they've partnered with as investors or board members.

It's critical to remember that VCs are not angels (no pun intended) and neither are they evil - they are investors whose job is to generate financial returns for their Limited Partners. VCs' interests will be aligned with the interests of founders as long as the founders keep making decisions that grow the value of the company. As soon as that is no longer the case, it is likely that VC's and entrepreneur's paths will diverge.

Before you start pitching to investors, sit down and create a list of VCs that write checks to companies at your stage, in your area of focus, and do not yet have competitive bets in their portfolios. Once you have the list, categorize all firms into three groups - A, B, and C. In category A, include the dream investors you would love to see on your cap table. In category C, list your worst-case options you will accept if everyone else says "no". Put everyone else in group B. When you are ready to start pitching, first reach out and talk to those in group C. Chances are you will be quite bad at first, but as you talk to more VCs, you will learn, get feedback, and iterate on your story. After going through the C list, you can start reaching out to those in group A. Since you only get one chance to make the first impression, you will want to be prepared when talking to your dream investors, and taking this approach helps you do it well (and potentially get a few term sheets along the way).

As you are sorting through hundreds of VC firms, you should know that although they may look the same from the outside, in many cases the way they operate, add value, support their founders, and encourage companies to grow are vastly different. Always start by thinking about the kind of business you want to build as that will inform what VCs could be the best fit. If you are selling to banks, VCs based on the East Coast are more likely to have connections in that field, and some will even have financial institutions as their Limited Partners. If you are building an application security company, firms in the Bay Area might be a better fit, and if your startup is selling to the government, you should try to find firms that have connections to the public sector.

Another thing to keep in mind is that VCs talk to one another a lot, share their impressions, and send one another pitch decks of the companies they are talking to, as well as those they passed on. This is especially the case in mature ecosystems such as Silicon Valley and Tel Aviv. When you are ready to start fundraising, you will want to time it in such a way that you take all the VC calls at the same time, and establish a deadline for term sheets. You have to be reasonable and read the situation, but you want to avoid dragging the fundraising process for weeks and months. You don't want your pitch deck to circulate for months and months because that sends a clear message that others have passed, and doesn't help you with closing the round. The longer you are raising the funding round, the less likely you will be successful. Unlike building a company, a successful fundraising campaign should be a well-planned sprint, not a marathon.

New entrepreneurs frequently get too enthusiastic after their calls with investors because a VC called their company "interesting" and said that they "believe in its success". Experienced founders know that there are only two potential outcomes from a conversation with a VC: they either write a check, or they don't. When you hear that it's not the right time, that they are still thinking, that they need some time to see how the market develops, take it as a "no", regardless of the stated reason. Process their feedback (if you can get them to provide one) and use it to challenge your assumptions but remember that fundraising is not a beauty pageant and you are not trying to convince everyone you are the best. All you need is to find an investor or two willing to work with you on good terms and give you the support you require.

Experienced VCs rarely say "no" and most definitely they don't burn bridges: they are well aware that what looked like an odd idea when no one else was interested in it, can become a hot startup when a top-tier firm develops conviction and wants to write a big check. Moreover, founders pivot, and a startup that was going into nowhere yesterday, may become the fastest-growing venture in town tomorrow. Good VCs say "not now", and it's up to founders to get as much feedback as possible. Asking for generic feedback after the investor decides not to invest isn't as helpful; what is much better is doing it after the pitch, before the decision is made. A question I find useful is "If based on what you learned you were to decide not to invest at this time, what would be the number one factor for that decision?". If it's too late, and the VC decides to pass, it is still possible to get good feedback, but you will have to be very focused. One way to do it is to ask "What is one thing that is most concerning about our company?". Do not try to convince them they are wrong; take this as a learning and be grateful for the experience. There is nothing that makes VCs doubt their decisions more than a founder who remains calm, respectful, constructive, and forward-thinking after they are told "no".

Venture firms don't just look for good companies, they want to fund the best, the most promising, the most desired startups. For that reason, they use interest from other investors in their portfolio companies as a sign that they made a good decision. Although getting funding is important, don't get stuck in the game of optimizing your business for VCs: it's customer love that will usually make or break your startup, not the investor's interest.

An important point to make is that venture capital is all about people - the specific partner you get to work with is much more important than the firm. At the same time, they may leave for another VC firm and you won't get to choose who ends up becoming your liaison or who joins your board if you have one. Make sure to choose investors you work with wisely and evaluate both the firm and its partners.

Expert Insight

"As a founder, you should think about selecting investors not only to secure capital but also to assemble your next set of close collaborators and partners. It matters just as much who you partner with as what they offer you. Picking the right partner is as or more important as picking the firm. While there are firm-level factors that influence behavior, the relationship between a founder and an investor is deeply important. Ask yourself, is this person going to challenge me? Point out my blind spots? Are they going to be empathetic? Mission-driven? Collaborative? Are they going to show up? Before you get too deep into negotiations with a VC, it may be worth calling a few references and getting together for dinner or coffee and seeing if they can pass the 'airport test'".

- Harpinder 'Harpi' Singh, Managing Partner at Innovation Endeavors, previously Co-Founder and CEO at Slice

Expert Insight

"Founders rarely know how to use their board or what to expect from them. To be fair, most boards don't know how to fix this problem, which is probably why the problem is so common.

Board members should be thought of as resources that the founder and the company can task and call on for help. In my experience, board members are huge supporters of the company and the founders. Unlike most anyone else, they've paid to be part of the business and are keenly interested in seeing it succeed. Sadly, many founders see the board solely as an audience to whom they periodically report.

The value which any given board member can provide will vary widely but successful founders figure that out. Ideally, they select their investors and board members based on their ability to help. And, great founders actively use these resources. They have no reluctance in asking the board for help and developing plans that include their participation."

- Mark McGovern, Venture Partner at Sands Capital Ventures

Raising money from corporate VCs

As we discussed before, different corporate VCs are motivated by different factors: some are looking for strategic alignment with their parent company, others purely for financial returns, and many for a combination of the two. When considering investment from a CVC, you will want to understand how they operate, the value they offer, and how they typically work with their portfolio companies.

One factor to keep in mind is that regardless of the CVC's motivations, you need to be strategic. Ask the partners of the CVC if they have experience getting their parent company to become a reseller or a customer of their portfolio companies. Look for examples of that in action: if they made it happen before, chances are that they will be open to doing it for you after they invest, but if they haven't, there is likely no system in place to make their ideas and great intentions possible.

Right way to approach fundraising

As you are going through the fundraising process, remember that the goal isn't to meet every investor; it should be to raise the amount of money you need on terms that are acceptable to the company so that the team can go back and focus on building the business. Although raising capital may not be what most founders set out to do when they dreamt about changing the world, it is a necessary step in building a company. Early-stage startups should never try to outsource fundraising to third-party representatives, intermediaries, or investment bankers. Through pitching and refining the message, you will learn and gain a broader perspective on your direction. Listen to the feedback and calibrate your understanding of the problems: VCs see hundreds of decks and talk to tens of founders weekly, so they have a broad perspective and know what is happening on the market, and what other people are building. At the same time, remember that it's you, not them who is the expert on the problem you are solving, and the customers you are solving it for.

As you go through the process of raising capital, you will want to surround yourself with people you can reach out to for advice. Having a strong support group is critical: reach out to other founders in your network, and most definitely consult with legal counsel experienced in startup fundraising. I would also recommend reading "Venture Deals", a book by Brad Feld and Jason Mendelson that covers a lot of the critical ground for those embarking on the fundraising journey.

Who you take the money from often matters more than the money itself. I have seen founders especially those who go through the accelerators culminating in demo days taking money from any investor who reaches out and says that they are interested. I think that is a mistake and entrepreneurs should be wiser when giving away ownership in their company. Although returning to building and selling as soon as possible is great, you also want the right people to support you. Founders may interact with contributors for a decade or more; your values, beliefs, ambitions, and vision of the future must be aligned. This is especially critical if the investor is going to lead a round and get a board seat.

Keeping investors in the loop with a newsletter

One tactic founders can use to build relationships with investors, advisors, and industry leaders is sending a regular newsletter with company updates. To find the best cadence, think of a timeline that will allow you to show good progress and stay top of mind for people you want to build relationships with. Most founders send monthly, bi-monthly, or quarterly emails. Here are some things you can include in the newsletter:

- A brief highlight of the most important news, such as partnerships, new customers, revenue, growth metrics, key hires, and press coverage.
- A short pitch of the company mission, and its key differentiators.
- Milestones the company has attained, and the goals it is pursuing.
- The key asks that make it easy for the company's friends to offer help (make them as specific as possible!).

While having this kind of newsletter is a perfect way to keep the friends of the company informed about the progress, it is especially useful for nurturing relationships with investors. It's a great practice to send it to both the VCs who are interested in the company, and those who have passed on the deal. It's surprising how many people end up eventually changing their minds when they see that the startup is moving fast, seeing a lot of interest, and hitting the numbers that matter.

Expert Insight

"For a first-time founder, navigating the nuance of fundraising can be overwhelming. After raising over $100M during the last bull market, I learned the following lessons of the process.

***Intentionally pick your angels**: Allocate equity only to angels that you will literally pick up the phone and call for advice. The biggest advantage with angels is that they are often not judgmental and you can be more candid with them than your board. Opt for angels who have either recently exited or are currently operating security companies, as the freshness of their operational insights tends to be the highest. Investors (VCs and angels) are not only designed to fund your business, but most importantly, to save you time by preventing common mistakes. This is why choosing people who are familiar with your space and* *have a network of security founders is crucial. You should also choose angels based on the stage of your company at a given time period. For example, if you are scaling the business, find a founder that recently went beyond $50M of ARR and is 1-2 stages ahead. If you are building the first product, find someone who did it recently and found their first 20 customers.*

Setting a valuation: *Early-stage startup valuations tend to be based simply on the amount of capital raised and a dilution amount. For example, it's typical for a Seed stage company to take about 15-20% of dilution, and if you are raising $5M, typically the valuation will be around $25M. In this stage, valuations are simple. As you start getting a cohort of paid customers, it becomes based on your growth rate, a multiple of your Annual Recurring Revenue, and other simple metrics.*

Keep VCs in similar stages during fundraising: *As fund-raising progresses, you will invariably get closer and closer to a term sheet. All founders want multiple term sheets for the highest chances of getting the best deal. As such, when you are talking to multiple VCs, keep them at similar 'stages' of the process, such as the initial pitch call or meeting the partnership. If a new one comes along during the late stages, politely let them know that you are far along in the process to set the right expectations. Some may be open to moving faster to get the deal, while some aren't."*

- Jack Naglieri, Founder and CEO of Panther Labs

Expert Insight

"Sharing some of my learnings based on the multiple rounds of funding for my startup as well as being an angel over the last few years.

The most important learning founders must keep in mind

is to always ***choose the right partner over the firm****. Having someone who has hands-on experience as a founder or has taken other companies through the same journey as an investor, and shares your values is super important.*

Always have at least one VC who specializes in the security space*. Their experience and learnings about the ideal customer profile (ICP), go-to-market strategy, marketing, team composition, and eventually exits can be very valuable and shorten your learning curve.*

Fundraising is a journey, so start building relationships early*, share updates, seek guidance, ask for intro to customers, and talent. This is also a great way to evaluate how much value an investor can add, and for investors to get to know the founders personally.*

Make sure you are transparent and aligned on the vision*, both about the type of business you want to build, the timelines, and the outcome. This will help you avoid a lot of pain and frustration later on. Not every company is destined for an IPO, so closing the right size VC partner based on the type of business is critical.*

Always raise more capital than you think you will need*. Things always take longer than you anticipate, and when they finally happen they always happen faster than you expected. Be ready to go all in and push the pedal and have investors who are willing to support you in your journey."*

- Prithvi Rai, Founder and CEO at Borneo

Designing business and distribution models

It doesn't take long to notice that most cybersecurity startups seem to lack imagination: they all attempt to sell in the same way it has been done for years, by getting CISOs into a demo and hoping security leaders will instantly realize just how awesome their "next-gen widget" is. Seemingly, there are no alternatives to this model: the only other way is to do product-led growth, but that has proven to be even harder to rely on. This is where most conversations about the go-to-market tend to end even though this is where the real story begins.

Although cybersecurity is everyone's problem, security companies don't get the ability to build for consumers and move up to enterprise customers, and vice versa. There are some exceptions such as password managers, but for the most part, a solution needed for individuals (all-in-one personal security) looks very different from what's needed for SMBs (all-in-one business-level security) which is even more different from what's required by the enterprises (advanced solutions to specific problem areas such as endpoint security, cloud security, etc.). Security startups have no choice but to pick a market segment they want to focus on from day one.

Three buyer personas and ways to sell to them

There are three types of customers: individuals, small and medium-sized businesses (SMBs), and enterprises, and they all have unique ways in which they evaluate and buy security tooling.

Regardless of whether or not people care about their security, one thing is clear: they don't want to pay for it. Of all the consumer-focused security products, only virtual private networks (VPNs) have gained mainstream adoption that compels people to pay for them. The reason for this has little to do with security though: individuals get VPNs to watch pirated movies and stream films outside of the US, and in some countries, to watch adult content and access sites blocked by the censors. In recent years, there has been a push for the adoption of password managers which started the trend of offering bundles for individuals even though most such companies derive the majority of their revenue from businesses. B2C security startups find that getting enough consumers to adopt security tools is an uphill battle.

Small and medium businesses are a huge part of the global economy. In the US, the numbers are staggering: according to the US Chamber of Commerce, there are 33.2 million small businesses (businesses that employ under 500 people) in America, which combined account for 99.9% of all US businesses. It gets better from here as the same report states that "Small businesses are credited with just under two-thirds (63%) of the new jobs created from 1995 to 2021 or 17.3 million new jobs. Small businesses represent 97.3% of all exporters and 32.6% of known export value ($413.3 billion). They also employ almost half (46%) of America's private sector workforce and represent 43.5% of gross domestic product". While SMBs have been greatly underserved compared to the enterprise market, achieving success in this segment is anything but easy. Some SMBs, especially those that employ 100-500 people, tend to be on the more mature side, but the vast majority have either low or no understanding of security and, subsequently, no budget for cyber defense. Selling to small and medium-sized companies requires a lot of education and a unique business model & unit economics that can guarantee profitability despite the low scale of deployment.

The vast majority of cybersecurity product companies target the enterprise market - a Holy Grail of the security industry. There are several reasons why this is the case:

- Presence of the budget - large enterprises have data to protect, and as such they are willing to allocate money to security.
- Regulatory requirements - in the effort to protect the public and strengthen the nation's defenses, the regulators are constantly raising the bar for what it means to secure the enterprise which generates demand for new security tools.
- Deal sizes - the large scale of deployment at the enterprises results in large deal sizes making them very attractive to the startups (one Fortune 100 customer can bring more revenue than 500-2,500 SMBs).

Historically, what has been working well is selling directly to security leaders - CISOs and CSOs or relying on channel partners (resellers, integrators, consultancies, and service providers). Because of the ever-growing number of security tools, CISOs of large enterprises have learned to rely on help and advice from industry analysts - companies such as Gartner, Forrester, and IDC. Subsequently, it became a part of the game for startups to invest in analyst relations to try to influence analysts' opinions. Over the past several years, new startups started struggling to stand out from the crowd and get noticed in the cacophony of the market, and the traditional go-to-market strategies have started to falter.

Thinking about the buyer's journey from the first principles

Many founders I have met think that building a company in security makes their go-to-market entirely pre-determined. "We are a B2B startup so we're just going to sell to the enterprise, get a CISO into a demo and show them how awesome our solution is". Or, they get too excited about the alternative and decide to embrace product-led growth, hoping that security practitioners will discover their tool on their own, and after the initial "Wow!" they'll immediately bring the product to their manager & get them to buy it on the spot. In my view, neither of these approaches is suitable for building a successful go-to-market strategy in today's market conditions.

To plan a winning go-to-market strategy, it's important to start by understanding the problem the company is trying to solve, identify who cares about seeing it solved the most, how they learn about the new solutions, and what factors and stakeholders impact their decision-making.

Even though the buying journey is rarely linear, it's unhelpful to think about it as a complicated mess. To make sense of the complexity, it's useful to do the buyer's journey mapping. There are many great templates online for entrepreneurs to use. Regardless of which one the founders choose, they will want to:

- Identify who is involved in the decision, what their power to influence the decision is, and what their interests are.
- Understand where people who are the most influential in the buyer's journey get their information; this is where you should prioritize your sales & marketing efforts. Although this step may sound basic, it's incredible how many companies invest in social media ads and campaigns when their money would be better spent organizing an invite-only event,

producing a useful report, or sponsoring their local BSides.

- Brainstorm the questions prospective customers are trying to answer at every stage of their buying journey, factors that may cause them to churn, their concerns, and motivations.
- Understand what activities prospects go through at every step of the journey (demos, internal reviews, budget approval, etc.).
- Develop a plan on how the company is going to address the needs of different stakeholder groups at each stage of their buyer's journey.

Mapping the buyer's journey is a useful exercise as it helps founders understand how their target market behaves and what people and companies need to become happy customers. Most importantly, it enables them to identify and test different go-to-market strategies because everyone who is a part of or can influence the buying process can be turned into a distribution channel.

Designing business and distribution models means starting from the first principles, generating hypotheses about what could work, and methodically trying different options to see what does. Then, doubling down on what brings the results and scrapping what doesn't.

Follow the customers: business model generation and different ways to sell security

Every startup is unique and there are no secret recipes for go-to-market success. What's important is that founders keep an open mind and look for ways to figure out distribution early. The list that follows isn't meant to be neither exhaustive nor prescriptive; it is here as an inspiration to show that there are different options and ways to sell security.

Going niche in B2C: some people do care about security

Although it is true that the vast majority of individuals do not care about their security, some do. A good strategy for B2C security sales is focusing on the niche categories for whom digital safety is critical for preserving their wealth, health, reputation, and even survival. The list includes journalists, human rights activists, politicians & other dignitaries, TV and movie actors, executives, high-net-worth individuals, adult industry actors, and sex workers, to name some.

It may be hard to build a growing business by going so niche, but it can be a great start. People for whom security isn't optional, are typically the early adopters of consumer-focused privacy and security tools.

Mastering B2B2C: security for individuals paid for by companies

There are two obstacles to consumer adoption of security products:

- Security adds friction, and people don't like to deal with friction if they can avoid it.
- Security costs money, and people aren't used to paying for software.

While the former cannot be effectively addressed within this discussion, the latter can.

One way to increase the likelihood that people will pay attention to security is to offer it for free. Instead of monetizing user data, there is another solution more suitable for selling cybersecurity, namely having the employer pay for it. This model, commonly known as B2B2C (business-to-business-to-consumer) has started to take off in the past few years. Some companies package their offerings as an "all-in-one security for executives", while others pitch security as an employee benefit. In both cases, it's an employer that pays the bill, not an employee. The hope is that once an employee leaves the job, they will most likely continue to pay for access to the tool or get their new employer to do it for them since it already has their valuable data.

When security is offered to individuals as an employee benefit, it comes from the benefits budget. This enables security products to be sold to human resources and people and culture departments instead of CISOs. The downside of this approach is that security as an employee benefit is a non-essential business expense, and as such it is more likely to go away during the budget cuts. However, once adopted, I'd assume (with no data to back it up) that most companies will continue to pay for employee benefits because no one wants to go to the people with the message that online security no longer matters.

Doubling down on the channel: giving the channel what it needs to sell

As previously mentioned, more than $9 of every $10 of cybersecurity sold goes via partners. Not only that: according to the research firm Canalys (https://canalys.com/), in Q2 2023, the growth of cybersecurity technology spending through the channel grew 12.7% far outstripping the 0.6% growth of direct sales. Also,

- Two-tier partners via distributors accounted for 69.3% of total spending. One-tier partners represented 22.2%.
- Resellers were the largest channel category, followed by systems integrators. MSSPs were the fastest-growing category followed by service providers.

Startups looking to sell through the channel often make a mistake assuming that all they need is to get in front of the resellers and integrators and demonstrate how great their solution is. The reality is much more complex.

To get started with the channel, startups will need:

- Proof there is a real demand in the market for what the company is offering. A demo and a few testimonials aren't enough: channel partners will expect that the startup will bring several finalized big deals, essentially giving them free money to start building relationships and show the market potential.
- Sales and customer enablement collateral, training, and constant feedback to make it easier for the channel sales reps to sell. Startups need to hire someone who is fully dedicated to fostering relationships, answering questions, providing training, checking in frequently, and doing anything that needs to be done to keep the sales reps engaged.

- Relationships with the salesforce and the right incentive systems. Providing collateral and hosting webinars isn't enough to keep salespeople in the channel engaged and motivated. Companies will have to invest in building relationships, recognize great performance, and treat the channel as an extension of their own team.

Companies need to think about the potential to sell through channel strategically, and early on in their journey. Some decisions, if made without consideration for channel sales, can close the door to this distribution method entirely. For example,

- If the company lists its pricing transparently on its website, it will be hard for resellers or integrators to charge the price they need to meet their margins.
- If the product is too cheap compared to the competition, channel partners who make a percentage of sales will not have as much incentive to actively promote the solution. A 10% of $1,000,000 is ten times more than a 10% of 100,000 ($100,000 vs $10,000); everything else being equal, salespeople in the channel are incentivized to sell more expensive products and services.
- If the product is hard to implement, or if it requires too many manual configurations to start going, channel partners are not likely to be as successful selling it compared to an easy-to-configure, out-of-the-box solution.

Expert Insight

"Channel distribution is the most potent growth vehicle for cybersecurity. Unlocking channel growth through partnerships starts from the fundamental principle of understanding how you can maximize partner revenues and gross profit margins. Hyper-scalers relentlessly pursue compute consumption, service providers strive to optimize service profit margins, and distributors absorb new solutions to expand their global price list for new cross-sell and upsell opportunities.

You're enabling a partner to launch a new line of business, but without having the constraints and overhead costs the partner does. Attack it bottom up, enabling their sales arm, and top down, guiding leadership to a new crop of opportunity. Focus on things that don't scale with an initial set of partners, then you can iterate and repeat at scale."

- Stan Golubchik, Co-Founder and CEO at ContraForce

Betting on the new type of channel: selling via data platforms

Data gravity (the ability of data to grow mass and attract products and services) leads to the tectonic shift in cybersecurity: security data is moving to Snowflake, BigQuery, Microsoft Azure Data Warehouse, Amazon Redshift, and the like. In the next decade, data warehouses and cloud providers have the potential to grow into the largest distribution channel for cybersecurity. Customers who already have their data in one place will find it easier to simply "enable" a capability that will then seamlessly plug into their data, instead of having to go through lengthy deployments and trials.

Security companies capable of getting their foot in the door and building partnerships can sell their offerings entirely through this channel. Field sales representatives for data lakes and cloud providers, equipped with marketing collateral and information about cybersecurity solutions, can upsell and cross-sell their existing customer base with little effort. Data warehouses and cloud providers track two metrics, storage and consumption; or to put it differently, storing the data and ensuring that customers use as many add-ons and services as possible to fully leverage the capabilities of the platform. Selling cybersecurity on top of their core offerings can drive consumption, help sales reps hit their quotas, and provide all sides with steady streams of revenue.

Working with ambassadors: reaching SMBs via vCISOs

Global cybersecurity sales in the SMB market category are estimated at more than $40 billion and according to some projections, should reach $90 billion by 2025. All this makes small and medium-sized enterprises an attractive market for cybersecurity founders. Selling to SMBs directly is hard as it requires educating them about their needs, ensuring they have enough budget, and so on. One other way to reach small and medium enterprises at scale could be by targeting another growing part of the security community - vCISOs.

Virtual CISOs, often referred to as CISOs as a Service, are security leaders who work with several organizations at the same time, doing similar work a full-time CISO would do (security strategy development, security & compliance program design, tool selection, and so on). I anticipate that the ever-rising pressure on CISOs, the growing number of regulations, and cases when CISOs are held liable and tried in a court of law for doing their job, will push more and more CISOs to leave their full-time jobs and become vCISOs. Today, however, most vCISOs are security practitioners who have never served as full-time CISOs and who are leveraging the vCISO role to learn the ropes of security leadership and potentially move into a full-time role at an enterprise in the future.

The vCISO community has the potential to become a powerful distributor of security solutions. vCISOs will need to diversify their sources of income and go beyond consulting, and working with vendors willing to pay sales commissions to get customers to adopt products that solve their problems can be a win-win for all parties.

Aligning incentives: B2B sales by partnering with insurance providers

Insurance companies are greatly incentivized to do what they can to prevent their customers from suffering cyber incidents. One way they do it is by mandating that policyholders purchase, maintain, and periodically upgrade their security products and services coverage.

The degree to which insurance companies are willing to recommend certain vendors varies: some maintain lists of "approved" or "preferred" solutions, while others adopt more of a principle-based approach and accept any tool that checks a list of predefined boxes. While most cyber insurance providers are more likely to suggest to their policyholders to buy security from established industry leaders, given the number of insurance firms, startups can find a way to build relationships with some of them.

For service providers, partnering with insurance companies may be even more straightforward. Insurers do not have in-house cybersecurity expertise, and therefore they rely on third parties for incident response (IR) and recovery when breaches inevitably happen. Savvy digital forensics and incident response (DFIR) firms may find partnering with insurance companies to be a great way to expand their reach and find a steady supply of customers.

Doing product-led sales right: turning security practitioners into ambassadors

There are many debates about product-led growth (PLG) and whether it can work in cybersecurity. The way I think about it is simple. First, in a market where several thousand vendors are fighting for the attention of the same security leaders trying to get them into a "quick 30-minute demo", it is highly unlikely that a new startup is going to succeed by doing what everyone else is doing. Second, startups do not have the resources to do white-glove onboarding or manually configure a test environment for every prospect. Anything that can be done to automate signup and onboarding will greatly help the company scale. Third, security products have always been known for having poor design and for being not user-friendly, so any company that builds an intuitive, easy-to-navigate tool will automatically earn respect in the community.

The ability for practitioners to easily try a security solution without having to go through several sales calls will continue to become more and more important. At the same time, I do not believe any company can build a business in security by simply doing PLG:

it's a great supplementary growth channel, but not the one that as of today can result in a successful stand-alone growth vehicle. Moreover, the leads generated by the product should still be sent to sales for follow-up, so PLG in cybersecurity is really product-led sales (PLS). Founders have to be mindful of this and temper their wishful thinking that they just need to build the product and the customers will come because in most cases, they won't.

Deep Dive

To learn more about the ways to implement the elements of product-led growth in a cybersecurity startup (and how not to do it), check out a Venture in Security deep dive titled "PLG is not a boolean: practical advice for cybersecurity startups looking to embrace product-led growth". You can find it by navigating to https://ventureinsecurity.net/p/plg-is-not-a-boolean-practical-advice or by scanning this QR code.

Selling through adjacencies: IT, finance, engineering, legal, and other functions

Security budget is a part of the IT budget, so when IT solutions the company already uses start to offer security capabilities, security teams have little choice but to evaluate them first. The desire to avoid a sprawl of security solutions and consolidate tools is here to stay. Companies such as Microsoft know this and build their whole business strategy around bundling.

As the surface area of security grows, so does the number of use cases with somewhat unclear ownership. This absence of clarity creates an opportunity for founders to bypass, or supplement the traditional CISO outreach. Here are some examples:

- Software security solutions can be positioned and sold to the engineering teams as well as security teams (or bundled into the tools for engineers from day one).
- Data security solutions can be positioned and sold to the data science teams as well as security teams (or bundled into the tools for data scientists from day one).

- People security solutions can be positioned and sold to the human resources and recruitment teams as well as security teams (or bundled into the tools for HR and recruiters from day one).

Lastly, depending on the startup's value proposition, founders may find that people who care about it the most are located far outside of security. For example, startups that promise to save costs may find it easier to get looked at by CISOs if the information is forwarded from their finance department. This approach, as any other, has the potential to backfire. CISOs may feel like an external team is encroaching on their territory and therefore disregard the proposed solution altogether, even if the product could indeed be a fit to address their problems.

VC as a distribution channel: leveraging investors for customer growth

The economics of venture capital firms (the so-called two and twenty model) doesn't make them great customers, but their connectivity turns VCs into perfect distributors. Investors are eager to show that they are offering value beyond capital, and their operating budgets equal to 2% of the fund size make it hard to hire large portfolio support teams. This is especially painful for small funds. The key to success in turning VCs into distributors is reaching out with solutions that:

- Have the potential to solve a real problem for their portfolio companies.
- Allow VCs to pass the costs of the value-add down to their portfolio companies.

One type of business that satisfies these criteria and therefore has been enjoying great success leveraging VCs as distributors is recruitment firms. By partnering with VCs, recruiters get introductions to the VCs' portfolio companies. It's a win-win for all parties: investors get to show that they are actually helping their founders, recruiters get a great source of business, and entrepreneurs struggling to attract talent get a pipeline of qualified candidates who could be a great fit for their teams.

Account-based sales: from aggressive cold calling to offering value to people who can benefit from it

When it comes to the go-to-market strategies, how a company goes about trying or implementing something is more critical than what it does. A case in point is sales outreach, in particular the so-called cold calling when business development representatives, or BDRs, make phone calls to people who could be a good fit for what the company is offering to get them to attend demos.

Cold calling is not a cybersecurity invention - that is how B2B sales have worked for decades. However, because security leaders and practitioners appear to be especially vocal about cold calling, founders in the industry tend to pick a side: they are either all for doing more of it because it brings results, or unequivocally against it.

I have talked to many people in the industry, and what became apparent is that the problem is not cold calling, but the way it is usually done:

- BDRs do not segment prospects, so instead of calling or emailing a select few companies who could be a fit, they embrace a "spray and pray" mentality and contact people and businesses that have absolutely no chance of ever becoming customers.
- Sales teams do not do their research, building an understanding of what problems the prospect might be experiencing, which domain it operates in, and how to best approach its team.
- Sales representatives are being unnecessarily aggressive and disrespectful of people's time, not taking "no" for an answer.

There are better ways to sell security without fully rejecting the concept of cold calling. Some of the ways to do it include:

- Investing time in researching prospects, their interests, problems, and potential angles for outreach. Sending templated or bland AI-generated emails or using the same script for every call is certainly not the right way to do sales outreach.
- Reaching out to people using their preferred communication

channels, or better yet doing it in settings where they are more likely to be receptive to the message. One of the issues in cybersecurity sales is that startups are being too transactional, without understanding that by getting to know security leaders in a neutral environment and building relationships, they are much more likely to close the sale.

- Being respectful of people's time and being transparent about the reason they are being contacted. I have seen some founders lie about looking for product feedback, and as soon as the call starts, launch into an aggressive sales pitch. I have yet to see a single case when that turns out well for the startup and lands them a new customer.
- Understanding that enterprise customers don't buy products just because they've heard something interesting about a new approach. The goal should be to make them aware of what the startup is offering in a way that builds, not destroys trust. This way, when the organization's security team finally prioritizes the problem the startup is solving, it will reach out and do the proof of value (POV).

Expert Insight

"Marketing and selling to security teams is a different ballgame compared to sales, healthcare, or even IT teams. This comes down to the nuances of unique personas on the buying committee and the technical complexities of cybersecurity.

***Skeptical of new security solutions:** The majority of security buyers have been burned before by vendors whose products did not live up to their exaggerated claims.*

***Time-poor:** Security teams are extremely busy fighting constant fires. Too often, vendors waste their time with vague messaging and inefficient sales processes.*

***Diverse buying committees:** In the past, winning over a CISO did the trick. Now, rightfully so, security practitioners are increasingly involved in the buying committee. These are very different conversations for GTM teams to master.*

Community-focused: *When scoping out new solutions (often discovered through word of mouth), security personas like to do their own research before speaking to sales by checking for peer reviews and engaging with security communities (Slack, Reddit, Discord, or community events).*

Overwhelmed by constant outreach: *It's not uncommon for security personas to get a dozen cold outreach emails or phone calls daily. Many take to Linkedin to blast overly aggressive tactics.*

For cybersecurity startups, building trust and credibility with security buyers is paramount. While building a brand, you are lucky to get 30 seconds of a security buyer's time, so it's even more critical to minimize friction and put the needs of your buyers first. Using an outdated lead generation playbook with aggressive outreach tactics erodes trust, especially with security buyers. Yet, it's still a common tactic used by cybersecurity vendors. The buyer's journey for security teams is not rigid and linear. Collecting emails ('leads') from gated ebooks and events at the top of the funnel who show no intent to buy, then putting them into a spam-like email nurture sequence or handing them off to sales for dozens of calls, is no longer effective.

To create demand, marketing should partner with cybersecurity experts to publish valuable content that establishes your expertise as the trusted resource for your ideal security customers. This content should be free and available natively in channels where security buyers spend the most time (hint: the answer for startups is not gated ebooks). Before you publish any content, ask yourself if it would give your target personas a competitive advantage and if it's frictionless to consume when shared via word of mouth, on Slack channels, and in private communities.

Sales and marketing teams should optimize for how security teams actually buy: through word of mouth, partners, references within communities, and value-led content that builds trust. Here are some quick tips to get started:

Replace overhyped jargon like 'complete protection' for messaging with credible outcomes you can prove. Your homepage should be free of jargon, fluff, and false promises (e.g. 'eliminate risk') and get straight to the point.

Instead of only focusing on CISOs, empower security practitioners to champion your solution by making it frictionless for them to do their own research before speaking with sales via ungated product tours, demos, and technical content that describes how they would use your solution.

Security buyers are busy, so don't waste their time. Instead of sending several emails back-and-forth to manually schedule a meeting, make it easy for them to book their first call with you or sign up for a demo with an automatic calendaring tool integrated into the form.

Produce value-led content that puts security buyers first rather than content that mostly promotes your company. This content should be in the native format of the channels where your ideal customers spend the most time. Aim to create content that helps security teams do their jobs better, save time, or learn new skills. When they are ready to buy, they'll remember the value you have already provided the community and reach out directly or through a partner.

- Chas Larios, Vice President of Marketing at Anvilogic

Expert Insight

"Some people see building a new category as the holy grail of entrepreneurship and rightfully so. New ideas shape the world and change the way we solve problems. Innovation is needed everywhere but especially in the security space which, despite decades of innovation, remains inefficient. With the glory come the challenges and considerations we need to take into account to be successful. I would like to share some of my learnings of successfully building a new category.

It is easier to position your startup as a natural evolution of an existing category than marketing what you do as a 'new invention'. Security is highly saturated, and adding another category will add to the noise and require a significant market education (think about the amount of capital you raise!). You need to have a clear message around the problem you're solving, and, ideally, suggest which existing solutions you can replace.

A category creator has to overcome a first-mover disadvantage: paving the road is often slow, while followers can move faster on the road already paved. As a founder, you will have to constantly sense the market, ask for feedback, and adjust as you go. Don't fall in love with your ideas.

Everyone talks about product-market fit but that isn't all you need. Make sure to define your go-to-market fit - your ideal customer profile, ideal pricing, geography, or industry verticals. When creating a new category, you'll often have to design a new go-to-market strategy as well, and there may not be any good references from existing categories to use. Since creating a new category is already hard enough, try to make your go-to-market strategy as common as possible. Don't needlessly reinvent the wheel on how to sell and market your product.

Less is more. Offer a clear value proposition and focus on fewer problems to solve. It takes time to change a market and sell new ideas, which leads me to the next thing to consider: be humble. Stepping into a meeting with a security team and explaining why the entire market (them included) 'got it all wrong' and 'before your company existed nothing really worked' will raise more objections to new ideas than support".

- Guy Bejerano, Co-Founder and CEO of SafeBreach

Expert Insight

"One of the fastest ways for a cybersecurity startup to burn through cash is to hire a crew of salespeople before they should. Closing cybersecurity sales is hard, which is why even a handful of executed deals get people excited. It's okay to be excited (I'm excited just thinking about it!) but it's important to temper the excitement that an initial set of sales generates. A handful of sales is not a scalable sales process or a validated go-to-market.

Building out your sales requires focusing on what it really takes to identify opportunities, the steps it takes to close a meaningful percentage of them, and then validating that these efforts are repeatable. Successful companies build a sales machine over time. They develop multiple 'sales motions' as they learn what works, and what doesn't. They learn how to bring on new salespeople and train them. They get bigger by learning how to sell in different ways, to different personas, and against different use cases. They learn how to forecast what their success will be over time and how to manage their costs accordingly.

The key to success is staying focused on reality and your situation. Your initial few deals mean you're onto something. Now identify what you did right, what you've learned not to do, and iterate. It may be time to expand the team but make sure you're focused on building a repeatable sales machine, not just hiring salespeople."

- Mark McGovern, Venture Partner at Sands Capital Ventures

Navigating industry events

The importance of industry events in the post-pandemic world

Events play an important role in shaping the state of the industry and as such, they deserve an honorary mention. The global pandemic changed the way we do business - hire new employees, attend product demos, negotiate and sign contracts, and get venture funding, to name some. Things that were previously unimaginable, such as raising capital from investors located hundreds of thousands of miles away without ever meeting them in person, became the norm. All this, combined with the growing list of virtual conferences and online communities, has led many people to believe that face-to-face interactions are no longer important. This could not be further from the truth.

The pandemic has changed a lot in the way society operates, but it hasn't changed human nature. We can meet people online and work remotely, but to form trusted relationships, we still need a face-to-face connection. The need to spend time in person hasn't been replaced by computers. What changed is the order of things. Before, one would meet a new person face-to-face and stay connected via cell phone or social media to maintain the relationship, but today we meet people remotely and then get together in person with those we would like to build a deeper connection with.

In a world where we are bombarded by millions of notifications, questions, and social media requests, having a personal relationship is more important than ever. This is especially critical in cybersecurity where most CISOs and practitioners ignore cold calling, social media, and email spam, but are happy to chat about their problems at events, meetups, and industry conferences.

There are many reasons to attend events: to learn, to build relationships, to showcase the brand, to attract funding, to get product feedback, to find customers, and to spend time with potential acquirers, to name some. The question isn't whether or not to go to events (the answer should in most cases be obvious), but which events to attend, how to behave, and what to do in order to maximize the value of being there.

From the perspective of a cybersecurity founder, there are three types of events: practitioner-focused, CISO-focused, and vertical-specific. Each of them is worth discussing separately.

Making the most of attending practitioner-focused events

One of the factors that make cybersecurity unique is the passion one feels when attending an industry conference. Nowhere it is so apparent as at practitioner-focused gatherings. Many great events fall under this category such as ShmooCon, Art into Science (ACoD), DEATHCon, and Blue Team Con, but two of the most popular ones globally are BSides and DEF CON. Black Hat can somewhat fit into this category as well because the first part of the event - Black Hat Trainings - offers attendees deeply technical hands-on courses on various cybersecurity topics.

For cybersecurity founders, the best way to make the most of attending a practitioner-focused event is to give a talk. As a rule, these events do not allow anyone to pitch their solutions, but I would argue that any good cybersecurity practitioner turned founder can find ideas to share that are interesting, useful, broadly applicable, and not designed to promote a product or service their startup is building. The value of giving a talk is not in getting people to try whatever the company is proud of, but to position its founders as thought leaders, allowing them to share their learnings as practitioners, and get that coveted speaker badge (it is surprising how many conversations it can start!).

Most early-stage founders won't have the money to sponsor large cybersecurity events, but supporting local BSides is both the right thing to do and can be relatively inexpensive, depending on where the company is located. If the startup is too early to afford sponsoring, founders can get nearly as much value if they come as regular attendees.

Two of the main goals founders should be pursuing when attending practitioner-focused security events are learning and hiring. Blue Team Con or BSides may not be great for pitching solutions (especially if the startup isn't one of the sponsors), but what they can provide is invaluable learning. Security practitioners are happy to discuss their own and industry-wide problems, ideate about what can be done better, and look for ways to advance the art and science of their craft. By asking powerful questions and focusing on building genuine relationships while being intentional about their presence, early-stage entrepreneurs can turn practitioner-focused events into fantastic sources of insights.

Making the most of attending CISO-focused events

While practitioner-focused events enable founders to get the perspective of those doing the hands-on work and using the tools the startup is going to be building, CISO gatherings are a perfect place to understand the pain points, needs, and perspectives of the security leaders. To achieve market leadership, the company will need to make both personas - buyers and users - happy, so the desire of many founders who themselves are ex-practitioners to ignore CISO-focused events is a big mistake.

CISO-focused security events, which include Gartner Summit Conferences and Forrester Security & Risk conferences, are a great place to get insights into what security buyers care about, what their priorities are, and what keeps them busy during the day and awake at night. Events such as RSAC and Black Hat, among others, also have parts in the agenda dedicated to discussing problems of security leaders, even if the conferences themselves are focused on broader topics.

Similar to practitioner-focused events, the best way to attend conferences for CISOs is to come as a speaker. Aside from being put in the middle of attention, another benefit of taking this approach is the cost savings: events targeting CISOs can be fairly pricey, and getting a free speaker pass can enable entrepreneurs to save a lot of money. Needless to say, these conferences have a very high bar for speakers, so unless one has served as a CISO before, or has a truly unique insight to share, getting on the agenda may be quite hard.

For aspiring and early-stage founders, a great way to make the most of CISO-focused events is to do what's often called a "lobbycon" - to go where the event is held without specifically attending the sessions and buying the expensive conference pass. These conferences tend to be hosted at hotels and other venues where founders can grab a coffee or pre-arrange lunches and dinners with CISOs in attendance even if the entrepreneurs themselves don't have the tickets to the event. Organizing invite-only social gatherings for security leaders is another great way to create a casual environment conducive to building relationships, learning about CISOs' pain points, and identifying ways in which the startup could address them.

Making the most of RSAC for early-stage cybersecurity startups

RSA Conference™, or RSAC for short, is the largest annual cybersecurity event that brings together the entire cyber ecosystem - vendors, security leaders and practitioners, investors, channel partners, regulators, and analyst firms, to name some. RSAC has been around for over 30 years, gathering around 45,000 attendees every year.

Although participating in the conference doesn't come cheap, for most companies it is well worth it: if the value of an average contract is, say, $100,000 per year, then attracting a single buyer can cover the event cost, and then some.

Fortunately for early-stage founders, RSA Conference has a variety of ways to take part in the event at low to no cost, including:

- RSAC Early Stage Expo showcases new cybersecurity companies and provides founders with the opportunity to meet potential customers, investors, and partners. Up-and-coming startups that qualify get their own kiosk for a special price. What's especially great is that the Early Stage Expo is typically located separately from the main RSAC floor, which means that CISOs and practitioners who attend the area are more likely to be open to (or even actively seeking) working with new startups.

- RSAC Innovation Sandbox is a competition that brings together ten early-stage companies to compete for the coveted title of "Most Innovative Startup." Since there is no cost to enter the competition, this can be a fantastic way for founders to get visibility and build relationships with potential customers, channel partners, investors, or even acquirers.
- RSAC 365 Innovation Showcase is a monthly virtual program where cybersecurity experts and entrepreneurs discuss new developments, ideas, and approaches shaping the future of the industry.

RSAC isn't an event in a classical sense, it's a global appointment for security leaders all over the world. The truth is that a lot of important parts of RSAC happen outside of the Moscone Center, official and unofficial gatherings, and events sponsored by vendors and VCs. Instead, they happen in private conversations in the lobby of the W, Blue Bottle Coffee, Starbucks, private hotel rooms, coffee shops, and offices of VC firms conveniently located in downtown San Francisco, as well as at private lunches and dinners. It is at those invisible to an untrained eye events that contracts are negotiated, partnership agreements are sealed, and terms of financing are discussed. Away from public attention, founders, investors, channel partners, and other players in the ecosystem brainstorm go-to-market strategies, set in motion joint ventures, and kick off initiatives that define the future of the industry.

Smart founders and busy executives do not rely on the RSAC schedule and serendipitous interactions alone to get the most out of their time at the event. Instead, they reach out to those they want to meet weeks ahead, knowing that during this one time of the year, most people shaping the industry will be in San Francisco downtown, regardless if they're native to the area, or if they call other places home, be it New York, Tel Aviv, or London.

Expert Insight

"RSA Conference is where business happens. It is where you find a plethora of venture capitalists, CISOs, buyers and sellers all meeting up in one place.

RSAC is a great convener for just about anything you might be looking for in the cybersecurity world but what is the best way to 'rise above the noise' while there? How do startups, especially early-stage startups, find their footing?

Well, that depends on your goal. If you are looking for funding, exhibiting at the Early Stage Expo not only gets you in front of curious CISOs, but many venture capitalists who are looking for their next investments. Or, if your product is not commercially available, applying for RSAC Launch Pad might be a perfect opportunity to not only get in front of three venture capitalists, but also give you a platform to pitch your idea to a broader audience."

- Cecilia Marinier, Sr. Director, Innovation and Scholars at RSA Conference

Making the most of vertical-specific events

For many startups, practitioner- and CISO-focused events may be a great place to learn about industry trends, new approaches, and technologies, but not necessarily to find customers. Instead of doing what everyone else does, and getting a booth at large industry events, security entrepreneurs should approach their marketing from the first principles. This means developing an understanding of who their customers are, what events they attend, and where they are most likely to be receptive to evaluating new ideas and solutions. If the company is selling to large banks, an event for the finance industry may be a better place to talk to their prospects; if the startup is targeting medium-size enterprises, meeting them at their industry or sector-specific conferences may bring better results.

It's not about events but about what you do at the events

Attending events and conferences will only lead to good results if founders are intentional and prepared. Being prepared doesn't necessarily mean having a fully booked calendar; it is more about having a plan, and the ability to recognize an opportunity and be ready to act fast when it presents itself. Regardless of what stage their companies are at, cybersecurity entrepreneurs can find industry events a great place to grow their venture:

- Those at the idea stage can find events to be a great place to learn, meet potential co-founders, conduct problem and market discovery, validate their hypotheses, and even find early design partners.
- Founders with an MVP can do demos and gather feedback, learn what people who match their ideal customer profile think, and test different messaging to see what resonates with buyers.
- Entrepreneurs with ready-to-sell products can find new customers, resellers, or partners capable of supercharging their distribution channels.

SECTION 5

A practical guide to failing a cybersecurity startup

A practical guide to failing a cybersecurity startup

"Why do startups fail?" is one of the most commonly asked questions among anyone interested in building a company. At first glance, a lot has been written about this problem. However, wherever I go, I continue to see three problems:

1. Most of the analysis is based on consumer startups.
2. Most of the analysis lacks the context of the cybersecurity industry.
3. Cybersecurity founders repeat the same mistakes over and over again.

In this part, my goal is to offer a guide to failing a cybersecurity startup, highlighting reasons I have seen startups fail, and offering insights and advice to avoid failures.

Not understanding the difference between building a product and building a company

Most of the future cybersecurity founders get exposed to the industry through products - tools they use to do their jobs. This makes sense; as domain experts, they are paid to ensure that their organization is secure, and to do that they need to either build solutions in-house or use those provided by third-party vendors. When security practitioners run into a pain point with tools available to them, they naturally notice gaps, issues, and opportunities that can be solved by building a better product. Determined to make the problem go away, some decide to build open-source projects on the side and make them accessible to the community for free, while others choose to start a company.

What security practitioners don't get to see from the outside is that there are other factors critical to startup success such as hiring, building a team culture, solving human resources issues, running operations, managing payroll, marketing, and investor relations, to name a few.

Many practitioners who become startup founders tend to over-invest in building technology and under-invest in areas equally critical to the company's success - marketing, hiring, fundraising, operations, and finance. To reduce the chances of this happening, security practitioners interested in building their own company in the future can look for ways to get exposure to the inner workings of cybersecurity startups. Angel investing and advising early-stage founders can be great ways to do it.

Not knowing the broader context that influences their ability to succeed

Related to understanding building a product versus a company, many cybersecurity founders do not understand the broader market context which influences their ability to succeed. The cybersecurity industry is notoriously complex, and a lot of the intricacies can only be learned with time, through trial and error.

Startup founders and aspiring entrepreneurs can build the foundational skills to navigate the industry by being active in the community, staying curious, asking questions, embracing the long-term mindset, and intentionally expanding their network.

Some of the areas critical to understand include:

- The market, its composition, forces that impact its direction, players that operate in it, and how all of this fits together. This includes the worlds of insurance and government regulation, venture capital and three-letter agencies, the legal landscape, and the channel partner ecosystem. Each of these components has a unique role to play, and understanding how they all interact, where they are at odds with one another, and where they amplify one another's impact is key to successfully navigating the industry landscape and making sound business decisions.
- The types of buyers, their buying criteria, and buying journeys. Depending on the geography, cultural context, industry, size of the organization the startup is targeting, and other characteristics of the purchasing process, the company will need different strategies to succeed. Over and over, I see founders saying things like "We are selling to enterprises", which means little: a bank in New York is going to buy differently than a large tech company in Austin, and the people who can influence the process in the Bay Area scaleup are different than those who can expedite or stall adoption at a pharmaceutical giant in Chicago. Not understanding the context and the buying journey can lead to a lot of waste, and ultimately a failed startup.
- The competition, its strengths, weaknesses, and the wedge it is trying to use. When asked about the competition, most cybersecurity founders I meet start talking about their products, highlighting how the solution they are building is superior, more scalable, more user-friendly, and more feature-rich than that of the competition. Unfortunately, as I've mentioned before, the product is not everything. Most of the time companies that appear to be doing the same thing, are built on different assumptions, target different market segments,

and acquire customers in different ways. Understanding the competitive landscape deeply is critical not simply to build a better product, but to craft and execute a business strategy that has a higher chance of winning.

Having unrealistic expectations about distribution channels and customer adoption

The biggest challenge of cybersecurity startups is not the product but its distribution. There are no right answers, but there are plenty of wrong ones. One of the most common mistakes I see cybersecurity founders make is focusing heads-down on building the product instead of allocating time to figure out distribution. Many in the field wrongly believe that the product will sell itself, without understanding that they are simply getting into the "We will build it and they will come" rabbit hole. While that is a relatively new issue, the "We will get a CISO into a demo" isn't. The unfortunate reality, however, is that most cybersecurity startups cannot turn cold calling and email spam into a viable growth strategy, especially if they are selling to security leaders at large enterprises.

There are options:

- Investor introductions. Those selling to CISOs should know that security leaders often buy products based on introductions from their venture capital networks.
- Security-adjacent functions. The ownership of several emerging areas of security is not clearly defined yet, which presents an opportunity for savvy founders to target people outside of the security team who can influence buying decisions.
- Channel partners and marketplaces. As the shape of the channel partner ecosystem is evolving, and the effects of data gravity create opportunities for cybersecurity vendors to develop new distribution partnerships, security founders may find new ways to acquire and retain customers.
- New ideas for distribution. Without trying to be prescriptive, I think it's important to highlight that the cybersecurity landscape is constantly evolving, which presents an opportunity to find new distribution ideas.

There are different ways in which security companies can distribute their offerings. To address the challenge of distribution, founders can pick a niche and become intimately familiar with the buying process, habits, and patterns in this niche. Moreover, they have to be realistic and understand that buying decisions are complex; a solid distribution machine is a must for any company looking to grow.

Scaling before the company achieves the product-market fit

Gauging product-market fit (PMF) in cybersecurity is much harder than in other industries. This is because in security, the creator of the solution is often educating buyers about the problem and creating the demand for what the company is building. In an industry where new attack vectors trigger the creation of new product categories, and market demand is often driven by government regulations, analyst firms, and catastrophic incidents, arguing what PMF is isn't easy. I see product-market fit as a state where the product is solving a commonly seen problem for a well-defined market segment so well that the customer is ready to pay for the solution, and there is enough demand to scale and build a company around it.

When a venture-backed company masters founder-led sales, finds the type of customer who is willing to pay for what it has to offer and confirms that it can do it repeatedly, then it's the time to start scaling. Unfortunately, what happens more often is that cybersecurity startups raise a lot of capital, hire large sales teams, and hope that by doing so they can get to the product-market fit quicker, bypassing the need to learn and iterate. This creates a deadly spiral where sales teams failing to hit unreasonable quotas start feeding product teams with "must-have" features, which turns the company into a feature factory. The startup becomes unfocused, promising everything for everyone, and burning capital faster than it can generate revenue. If despite all these challenges the company can preserve some focus and build a working product, it may still get acquired. Otherwise, it will have to conduct massive layoffs and hopefully do some soul-searching and iteration to get to the PMF. When the market is "hot", startups can access cheap capital and the pressure to be prudent is lower.

To avoid potential problems, cybersecurity entrepreneurs should continue learning and iterating quickly to get to the PMF before they start scaling the company. And, they must understand that just because they hired more salespeople, they won't automatically get more sales, especially if their positioning is not working, there is no PMF, the product is not meeting expectations around quality, etc.

Expert Insight

"It is super important for founders who are going from zero to one not to settle for a weak product-market fit before hiring more than one or two salespeople. It is a classic example where slowing down (in terms of revenue acquisition) to achieve strong product-market fit will help revenue acquisition grow much faster in the long run. Founders who raise money from VCs will feel pressure to show revenue growth as quickly as possible, but it can be a huge mistake when it leads to founders increasing spend on go-to-market before achieving a strong product-market fit."

- Kumar Saurabh, Co-Founder and CEO at AirMDR, previously Co-Founder and CEO at LogicHub and Co-Founder and VP of Engineering at Sumo Logic

Expert Insight

"Ultimately, a security startup needs two things. First, effective feedback loops, so that it can be aware of mistakes. Second, the agility and courage necessary to throw away what isn't working, and pivot to the next idea. Security vendors have more of an opportunity to pivot than most startups, and should use this flexibility to their advantage. A vendor with effective feedback loops, agility, and a leadership team that knows when to move the rudder can survive even the worst markets."

- Adrian Sanabria, host of the Enterprise Security Weekly podcast

Not assembling a team that has the chance to win

The composition of the founding team has a direct impact on how the startup is going to develop, and what challenges it is likely to encounter. Many security companies are started by two or three security engineers or domain experts who found the problem or identified an opportunity in the market and decided to tackle it. This is also the composition of the team often preferred by VCs, and for good reason; at the earliest stage, startup founders need to build the product and two people can ship code faster than one. Additionally, the argument is that cybersecurity is a technical discipline, so having all founders with deeply technical backgrounds is a good thing. Engineers are typically clear and logical thinkers, which makes them well-suited to take care of other sides of running the company, from operations to fundraising.

Despite the consensus that having several engineers start a company is a good idea, I have also observed a potential dark side of this approach. It's not uncommon to see that when things get tough and the company is struggling to acquire customers, the all-engineering founders retreat to the area they can control: the code. I have seen company founders doubling down on building new features when what they should be doing is selling, doing customer discovery, and deciding where to focus their efforts strategically. Instead of building the company culture, asking questions to understand what they might be missing, developing partnerships with other industry participants, and addressing other pressing issues, engineering founders often decide to build - more code, more features, more scale, etc.

On the opposite end, I have also seen what happens when a few business people with little to no understanding of the technical side of cybersecurity try to build a company in the security industry. The chances of this approach succeeding are low, and directly depend on the market segment founders choose to tackle. There is a difference between building a tool for compliance teams and a cloud security solution: the former can be done with business understanding alone, but for the latter, having deep technical expertise will be critical. What definitely won't work is having a person with no background in cybersecurity assemble a team of contractors to build a "next-generation, revolutionary solution" to solve a very complex, technical problem.

I believe that having a combination of technical and non-technical founders is ideal and that founding teams of 3-4 people are better than solo or even duo founders. If I were to build a cybersecurity company (or rather when it happens), I would be looking for engineers and security practitioners who can complement my expertise in product, go-to-market, sales, business development, positioning, operations, and fundraising.

Trying to be yet another "single pane of glass"

Being invisible in the enterprise stack does not sound as exciting as building "the only dashboard" that the security practitioner will be using daily. Most companies are driven by the desire to own the customer and eventually upsell them on new products, so cybersecurity is full of startups that want to be at the center of attention. As a friend once said, "Most security products want to become a single pane of glass but instead they become a single glass of pain".

There cannot reasonably be 50 dashboards a practitioner must interact with daily. Therefore, trying to go to market as "yet another single dashboard" is not a winning strategy for most startups.

Building features in search for a product

Many cybersecurity solutions start as single features which then grow into products. Every feature wants to be a product, and every product wants to be a platform. While it is true that innovation in the industry is most commonly acquired, not built in-house, some solutions are way too granular to have the ability to grow into something larger. And, if a big vendor can build the same feature or product in a month and a half, and the whole defensibility of the startup relies on the hope that it won't, it is probably not the best problem to build a company around.

Being too early or too late to the market

D'Arcy Coolican of a16z coined the term product-zeitgeist fit (PZF) which he describes as a state "when a product resonates with the mood of the times". I think every cybersecurity founder should understand this concept. Being too late to the market is bad, and we know that: building an endpoint detection and response (EDR) solution in 2023 is most likely a bad idea. At the same time, so is being too early, when the approach the company is proposing is too futuristic and many years ahead of the time. If you want to see an example of what that could look like, I highly recommend "General Magic" (2018), a documentary about one of the most impactful Bay Area companies the vast majority of people have never heard of.

In cybersecurity, there is the first entrant disadvantage because the company that champions a certain approach has to educate buyers about the problem. On the other hand, the first entrant can also enjoy enduring market leadership, if it can execute well. Knowing whether the pros of championing the new approach are going to outweigh the cons is an art, not a science.

Deep Dive

To learn more about product-zeitgeist fit, check out a Venture in Security article titled "To succeed, cybersecurity startups need to be triple fit". You can find it by navigating to https://ventureinsecurity.net/p/to-succeed-cybersecurity-startups or by scanning this QR code.

Not having a viable business model

Not every solution to an important problem can be a foundation upon which a successful company can be built. Moreover, not everything needs to be a business, and some initiatives are better off as non-commercial, accessible, free open source projects.

Founders interested in creating a company, whether or not they are looking to build a venture-backed startup, need to be intentional when thinking about the business model, unit economics, revenue channels, cost structure, distribution, and other factors that impact business success. Just because someone is buying a product doesn't mean that the company will be able to scale, if the unit economics do not make sense.

Expert Insight

"Companies that adopt land-grab strategies can secure a major advantage by being the first to dominate a large part of the market. This initial dominance can create hurdles for other startups trying to enter the same space, positioning the first company as a market leader. Quick scaling (even while not initially viable) can bring about cost efficiencies, lowering the price of each product or service. This reduction in cost can make the solutions more budget-friendly for users and boost the company's earnings in the long term, at the sacrifice of the short term."

- Jonathan Haas, Co-Founder and CEO at ThreatKey

Looking for consultants to craft the go-to-market strategy

I have seen several founders hiring consultants to "figure out the go-to-market". This is especially (but not exclusively) common when all founders are engineers who built a "great solution" and now they "just have to hire someone to figure out who needs it and why".

Cybersecurity entrepreneurs are the ones who know their product, their market, and their vision the best, and their success is most aligned with the success of the company. In 99 cases out of 100, outsourcing the learning and crafting of the go-to-market strategy to an external agency or a consulting group does not work. If the founders can't understand who needs their product and close deals, it's unlikely that someone else will.

Not being able to distinguish between selling to investors and selling to customers

Many tech companies repeat the same mistake: attempting to sell to their prospect the same way they sell to their investors. This is especially the case in cybersecurity where the vast majority of the market players are startups. Security founders must understand the difference between how these two groups make their decisions:

- Only ~10% of what the investor is buying already exists; 90% or more is yet to be built. VCs are buying a vision of where the company could (and hopefully - will) be. Selling to investors is about getting them excited, getting their eyes lit up, and imagine what may be possible tomorrow.
- Over ~90% of what the enterprise customer is buying must exist today; 10% or less can be a future vision. Buyers know that startups are inherently risky and unstable, and a year or two later the company may be gone - it will either get acquired, and the parent company will change the product, pivot its focus, or even go out of business. Enterprise CISOs want to know what problems the product will solve for them today. Selling to enterprises is about enablement, support, response times, contract price, product capabilities, the ability to replace parts of the current or legacy stack, and other pragmatic matters.

Expert Insight

"In my research, I've observed that the best products in security doesn't necessarily win the market. The most successful security companies had a decent product with an exceptional go-to-market engine.

Founders risk failure when they fail to think about the end-user experience and distribution when building out the product.

It's important to remember that increasingly CISOs prefer to handover products to their teams to test it before making the final decision, so if security teams or developers can try out your product without having the CISO be involved, this can create quick time to value which increases the likelihood of your product gaining momentum in the organization."

- Francis Odum, cybersecurity instructor & researcher, author of the Software Analyst blog

SECTION 6

Building security companies the world needs today

Do not build a company on autopilot

I think one of the biggest challenges in the cybersecurity startup space is that most founders are building a company on autopilot, taking the "market playbooks" as immovable rules to play by, and continuing to do what has been done by thousands before them, over and over. Some do it because they haven't seen the whole variety of options they can choose from, while others may be pressured by their investors and boards.

For example, too often I see founders update their social media pages to "Founder of a Stealth Startup", disappear from the public eye, drown in conversations with VCs, and spend months building and perfecting ideas before ever talking to customers. What if they could instead set their LinkedIn to "Founder of Company A" and start evangelizing about the problem area to build a community of followers and supporters without revealing the exact angle they are taking? Moreover, what if they raised a small amount from angels, avoided getting distracted by VCs, and started selling to the customers in advance, while quickly validating the problem area? Then, armed with all this validation and interest from companies who already agreed to become design partners, they could raise the capital they need with less effort and on better terms. This is just one example; there are many others.

Instead of building a company on autopilot, following the same path that has been repeated thousands of times with various degrees of success, cybersecurity entrepreneurs should keep in mind the problems they are trying to solve, both in the industry and for themselves, and rely on first-principles thinking to guide their decisions. Moreover, sometimes instead of hiring people who come not to learn but to execute their "playbooks", founders should be looking for high-performers willing to adopt the beginner's mindset and do what works. Not what worked for them a decade ago in another market or a different company, but what brings the best results today, in the specific problem area the startup is tackling, and for people it is selling to.

Expert Insight

"A select few founders will need to be willing to jettison conventional playbooks and re-imagine what and how technology works to really improve the security of technology. Abstracting, extending, and layering more things on top of the same old tech won't change anything. In our lifetime, the tipping point between being able to maintain the security of our longstanding compute architecture will be too difficult and threaten the benefits technology can have going forward."

- Nicholas Muy, CISO, operator, and investor

Going past playbooks when choosing problems to solve

When most people with expertise in cybersecurity think about problems in the enterprise, their minds immediately go to security teams. Although it makes sense, there could be other problem areas, such as privacy, physical security, fraud prevention, and the like that are security-adjacent, but do not have to be sold directly to CISOs. There could also be interesting problems outside of the enterprise space, such as detecting shoplifting in retail stores using computer vision - a security-adjacent challenge with a decent market size and potentially a strong demand.

Alternatively, founders could think outside of the box, exploring problems that are most pronounced in other domains and are not limited to security. For instance, security automation at its core is enterprise automation, and while security teams could be a great way to start, there is a clear opportunity to expand into other use cases later.

Going past playbooks when assembling teams

Most security companies are started by two co-founders who are either both engineers or one engineer and one focused on running the business. What if instead of adhering to this playbook, founders were more intentional and assembled teams to increase their chances of success?

I think about this a lot when looking at companies coming out of Israel. Oftentimes, Israeli security startups are founded by alumni of elite military units such as 8200, and backed by the country's top VCs who are also deeply immersed in the same networks. This model has worked well, creating tremendous value for both founders and investors. As the market is becoming more and more competitive, relying on the same playbooks is getting riskier. The challenge is that when everyone comes from a similar background, talks to the same people, gets the same advice, and develops the same strategies, it naturally limits the imagination. The new ideas are more likely to come from bringing together the perspectives of the leading Israeli entrepreneurs and combining them with those of the American, and global counterparts. I think that assembling diverse Israeli-US founding teams can create conditions for innovating business models, go-to-market strategies, and sales and marketing approaches. And, I think in the coming years we are going to see more and more of this happening.

Deep Dive

To learn more about the factors that played a critical role in turning Israel into one of the global leaders in cybersecurity and what the future may look like, check out a Venture in Security deep dive titled "Why Israel may become the winner in the global cybersecurity market, and what can make it fail". You can find it by navigating to https://ventureinsecurity.net/p/why-israel-may-become-the-winner or by scanning this QR code.

Going past playbooks when focusing on the go-to-market

The traditional playbook in security has been to sell directly to CISOs - cold call or cold email them in the hope of getting a demo and seeing what happens. What if founders could challenge this approach? First and foremost, if the potential value of the contract is millions of dollars, should we not be investing more time in learning who we are selling to, their needs, goals, and problems? Should we not be looking to build relationships and create "CISO magnets" that would make security leaders interested in talking to the company, instead of trying to get them trapped in a sales demo?

If we start by thinking about the target market and understanding the people we are selling to deeply, we can usually come up with better ways to reach them. What does our ideal customer profile look like? What do people who match it read? Where do they spend their time? How do they learn about the new developments in the industry? Starting with first principles can help entrepreneurs get out of their mental blocks and playbooks that have "always worked" and invent new ways of selling that deliver the right results.

To enable your mind to see new ways of solving old problems, ask yourself "What might we be doing if there was no option to sell to CISOs directly?". Framing it this way allows you to brainstorm and test all kinds of ideas - going through finance, legal or procurement; partnering up with service providers or vCISOs; partnering with insurance providers; selling through deputy CISOs and VPs of security and the like.

Challenging the playbooks around go-to-market goes further than this. What if instead of sponsoring the industry conference you could organize your own? What if instead of paying thousands of dollars to have your ad aired on a podcast you can build a community around your own podcast? Opportunities are plenty; we need founders daring to think differently to seize them.

Deep Dive

To learn more about the importance of thinking big from day one, check out a Venture in Security deep dive titled "A shortage of cybersecurity founders building companies, not features or products". You can find it by navigating to https://ventureinsecurity.net/p/a-shortage-of-cybersecurity-founders or by scanning this QR code.

Building security companies the world needs today

If there is one thought I'd like to leave you with it would be this - cybersecurity is changing, and we need people to build the companies the world demands today. This means being adaptable to changes, willing to experiment, and open to challenge the ways things have always been done.

The industry is maturing - more and more organizations are starting to hire practitioners capable of tailoring the generic defenses to the company's environment and architecting the systems in a way that when incidents inevitably happen they won't take down the whole business and will instead be contained and isolated effectively. More and more companies are starting to understand that security is a process, and not a product or a feature they can just "deploy" or "enable" and forget. More and more organizations are giving security practitioners a voice when it comes to tool evaluation and selection.

The changes are happening, but they are not and will not be as sweeping as some would like. As with anything else, we tend to overestimate the magnitude of changes in the short run and greatly underestimate them in the long run. I do think the industry will look differently tomorrow. However, founders starting today, have to both build for the industry that is emerging and for the industry they operate in today. They need to be grounded in reality but aspire to make this reality better over time. This means playing well with industry analysts and finding ways to work with channel partners. It means recognizing that the most mature companies - the power users - are a small subset of the market, and building products where advanced use cases are possible, but not mandatory to get value of the product. This means building solutions for the market where most customers don't have armies of security engineers and won't be getting them anytime soon.

One of my favorite quotes, attributed to Abraham Lincoln and Peter Drucker, says: "The best way to predict the future is to create it". In security, many voices are trying to predict the future; what we need are the hands and minds willing to do the hard work and build it. We need people crazy enough to do the work to push the industry forward, but smart enough to not get stuck in the echo chambers of investors, power users, and those who think that the industry will look the same in twenty years, "just with more consolidation". We need doers. We need dreamers. We need builders.

I hope this short book will help you make your contribution to help secure the future. I know it won't have the answers to all the questions you need answered but it wasn't my intent. My goal was to share the knowledge I accumulated working in the industry, organize the points I have previously shared in my blog, Venture in Security, and put together an essential guide about the business side of cybersecurity for builders - founders, engineers, practitioners, product managers and others creating the future of cybersecurity. If you have learned something valuable, please share it with others; if you know someone in your network who would benefit from having this book, please send them a link or give them a copy.

I am always looking for ways to support big ideas and big ambitions. If you're working on something that has the potential to solve an impactful problem - send me a message. And, if you are getting ready to take a leap and build, and looking for advice, a co-founder, or a perspective from someone with experience on the business side of the industry, please also say "hi". It's a small industry, and who knows what the future holds.

Onward! It's time to build.

Book Recommendations

Five essential books for cybersecurity startup founders

- If you only read one book, make it "The Hard Thing About Hard Things: Building a Business When There Are No Easy Answers" by Ben Horowitz
- If you only read two books, make "The Great CEO Within: The Tactical Guide to Company Building" by Matt Mochary, Alex MacCaw, and Misha Talavera be the second
- Core principles for life, work, and business: "Principles: Life and Work" by Ray Dalio
- To get into the mindset of creating a company that will shape the future, get "Zero to One" by Peter Thiel and Blake Masters
- Learn about ways to see if your business idea makes sense when everyone, your friends and people you ask, will just say nice things to make you feel good: "The Mom Test: How to talk to customers & learn if your business is a good idea when everyone is lying to you" by Rob Fitzpatrick

Think about the future of the industry

- Get a framework to identify where new opportunities in cybersecurity can come from and what to build: "Cyber Defense Matrix: The Essential Guide to Navigating the Cybersecurity Landscape" by Sounil Yu
- Reflect on the future of cybersecurity: "Rethinking InfoSec: Thoughts on why today's Information Security doesn't work, and how we can do better" by Greg van der Gaast
- Learn about influencing industry analysts: "UP and to the RIGHT: Strategy and Tactics of Analyst Influence: A complete guide to analyst influence" by Richard Stiennon

Raise capital

- Learn about raising capital from angel investors, how angels think and make decisions, and how to work with them: "Angel: How to Invest in Technology Startups-Timeless Advice from an Angel Investor Who Turned $100,000 into $100,000,000" by Jason Calacanis
- Learn about raising capital from VCs, how venture capital works, what makes a startup a fit for the VC model, how to structure the fundraising process, and what parts of the term sheet matter: "Venture Deals: Be Smarter Than Your Lawyer and Venture Capitalist" by Brad Feld and Jason Mendelson

Acquire customers

- Learn a step-by-step process to position your product, service, or company: "Obviously Awesome: How to Nail Product Positioning so Customers Get It, Buy It, Love It" by April Dunford
- Learn about the stages of startup growth, the types of users (innovators, early adopters, early majority, late majority, and laggards), and how to get your product beyond a small circle of early enthusiasts: "Crossing the Chasm: Marketing and Selling Disruptive Products to Mainstream Customers" by Geoffrey A. Moore
- Learn about ways to break through to new customers and grow your startup: "Traction: How Any Startup Can Achieve Explosive Customer Growth" by Gabriel Weinberg and Justin Mares

Build company culture

- Learn about giving feedback and building a culture of transparency: "Radical Candor: Be a Kick-Ass Boss Without Losing Your Humanity" by Kim Scott
- Learn about hiring the right people: "Who" by Geoff Smart and Randy Street
- Learn about dealing with team dysfunctions that commonly plague startups: "The Five Dysfunctions of a Team: A Leadership Fable" by Patrick Lencioni

Design your business model

- Learn how to experiment with and design new business models: “Business Model Generation: A Handbook for Visionaries, Game Changers, and Challengers” by Alexander Osterwalder and Yves Pigneur
- Learn practical frameworks for designing a viable business model, validating ideas & generating insights: “The Real Startup Book” by Kromatic
- Learn about building open source products: “Working in Public: The Making and Maintenance of Open Source Software” by Nadia Eghbal

Build a new product category

- Learn how to build a new product category: “Play Bigger: How Pirates, Dreamers, and Innovators Create and Dominate Markets” by Al Ramadan, Dave Peterson, Christopher Lochhead, and Kevin Maney

Build and scale your product

- Learn how to build an empowered product team, structure process, and prioritize what to work on: “Inspired: How to Create Tech Products Customers Love” and “Empowered: Ordinary People, Extraordinary Products” by Marty Cagan

Become more effective

- Learn how to build genuine relationships with people and form a community around yourself and your mission: “Never Eat Alone, Expanded and Updated: And Other Secrets to Success, One Relationship at a Time” by Keith Ferrazzi and Tahl Raz
- Learn about effective negotiation strategies for high-stakes conversations: “Never Split the Difference: Negotiating As If Your Life Depended On It” by Chris Voss and Tahl Raz

Amazon links for book list

You can find Amazon links to the books listed by visiting https://ventureinsecurity.net/p/book-recommendations or by scanning this QR code.

Additional Resources

For additional resources such as lists of cyber-focused investors, blogs, and online communities for security startup founders, visit https://ventureinsecurity.net/p/resources or scan the QR code.

Gratitude

There is a famous European folk story about stone soup. In this story, strangers start boiling a stone and then ask people in a small town to each bring one ingredient they have at home. At first, everyone is skeptical but as more ingredients are added, the soup starts to taste better and better. In the end, a meal that initially had one ingredient, a stone, turns into a feast that the whole town gets to enjoy. The fable shows the value of sharing and bringing what you have to the table to help others.

This book is a stone soup of its own. The only reason why I was able to learn so much about the industry is because everyone I met over the years was so generous in sharing their experiences, ideas, and perspectives. CISOs, founders, investors, security practitioners, industry analysts, service providers, resellers, and anyone I've spoken to were always open and willing to share what they knew. Most people who contributed to this book did so indirectly and without ever suspecting the impact of what they were doing, by having a good conversation at a conference, by sharing a link to an interesting article, and by hopping on a Zoom call. While I cannot list all of them (such a list would have been longer than this book), my gratitude to everyone who helped me on my journey is immense.

I want to say a huge thanks to Richard Stiennon because I don't think I would have gotten the courage to write this book without his encouragement. I am grateful to Valerie Zagarpur for helping me navigate the process of getting the book together and sharing a wealth of resources about publishing. I would like to say a sincere thank you to Caleb Sima and Jeremiah Grossman for writing forewords to the book. Furthermore, I am beyond grateful to Sean Sun, Ben Normanton, and the amazing Miscreants team for designing the book cover, and before that, the Venture in Security brand. And, I am thankful to Anshu Gupta for finding the time to read this book cover to cover, provide valuable feedback, and catch what felt like one hundred typos, errors, and omissions. Special thanks to layout designer and editor Scott McFarlane for his work on layout, styling, and final copy of the book, and for finding a way to integrate a variety of elements such as the "Expert Insights" and "Deep Dives" so they flow well for the reader. Without kindness and help from all these people, I don't think "Cyber for Builders" would see the light of day anytime soon.

Finally, I would like to express my sincere gratitude to a long list of people who contributed their thoughts to the book:

- Adrian Sanabria, host of the Enterprise Security Weekly podcast
- Allison Averill, Vice President at Unusual Ventures
- Andrew Smyth, Partner at Atlantic Bridge
- Anshu Gupta, CISO and angel investor, member of Silicon Valley CISO Investments
- Anthony Bettini, Founder and CEO at VulnCheck, previously Founder and CEO at FlawCheck and Founder and CEO at Appthority
- Austin Arensberg, Head of Okta Ventures
- Bob Ackerman, Founder and Managing Director at AllegisCyber Capital and Co-Founder of DataTribe
- Bryson Bort, Founder and CEO at SCYTHE, Founder and Chairman at GRIMM Cyber
- Cecilia Marinier, Sr. Director, Innovation and Scholars at RSA Conference
- Chas Larios, Vice President of Marketing at Anvilogic
- Chris Hughes, Co-Founder and President at Aquia, Cyber Innovation Fellow at Cybersecurity and Infrastructure Security Agency (CISA)
- Clint Gibler, the creator of tl;dr sec, a free weekly newsletter read by over 30,000 cybersecurity practitioners to CISOs, founders, and VCs
- Cole Grolmus, Founder and Author at Strategy of Security

- Corey White, Founder and CEO at Cyvatar
- Corin Imai, cybersecurity marketing leader, formerly a security researcher
- Dani Woolf, Founder and CEO of Audience 1st
- Dino Boukouris, Founder and Managing Partner at Altitude Cyber
- Dor Morgenstern, Senior Product Manager at Torq and Founder of the Founders Circle at 8200 Young Forum
- Eldon Sprickerhoff, Founder of eSentire
- Eric Capuano, Founder of Recon Infosec
- Fernando Montenegro, Senior Principal Analyst at Omdia
- Francis Odum, cybersecurity instructor & researcher, author of the Software Analyst blog
- Frank Wang, Lead Security Engineer at Headway and author of the Frankly Speaking blog
- Guy Bejerano, Co-Founder and CEO of SafeBreach
- Harpinder 'Harpi' Singh, Managing Partner at Innovation Endeavors, previously Co-Founder and CEO at Slice
- Idan Gour, Co-Founder and CTO at Astrix Security
- Jack Naglieri, Founder and CEO of Panther Labs
- James Green, General Partner at CRV
- Jimmy Mesta, Co-Founder and CTO at KSOC
- Jonathan Cran, angel investor at Resilient Thesis, previously Founder and CEO at Intrigue
- Jonathan Haas, Co-Founder and CEO at ThreatKey
- Jonathan Luff, Co-Founder of CyLon Ventures
- Kumar Saurabh, Co-Founder and CEO at AirMDR, previously Co-Founder and CEO at LogicHub and Co-Founder and VP of Engineering at Sumo Logic
- Kyle Hanslovan, Co-Founder and CEO at Huntress

- Lennart Koopmann, Founder of nzyme, previously Founder of Graylog
- Lior Yaari, Co-Founder and CEO at Grip Security
- Mark McGovern, Venture Partner at Sands Capital Ventures
- Maxime Lamothe-Brassard, Co-Founder and CEO at LimaCharlie
- Mike Privette, independent industry analyst writing at Return On Security, advisor, and angel investor
- Moty Jacob, Co-Founder and CEO at SURF Security
- Nicholas Muy, CISO, operator, and investor
- Nipun Gupta, Chief Operating Officer at Bearer, startup advisor, and angel investor
- Ofir Har-Chen, Co-Founder and CEO at a stealth-mode cybersecurity startup
- Oliver Rochford, product strategy advisor and former Gartner analyst
- Omer Singer, security strategist at Snowflake and Anvilogic
- Paul Caiazzo, Chief Growth Officer at SnapAttack
- Prithvi Rai, Founder and CEO at Borneo
- Ravi Ithal, Co-Founder and CTO at Normalyze, previously Co-Founder and Chief Architect at Netskope
- Richard Stiennon, Chief Research Analyst at IT-Harvest
- Rick Gordon, Co-Founder and CEO at Tidal Cyber
- Robert Kugler, angel investor and a member of the Cyber Club London (CCL)
- Sid Trivedi, Partner at Foundation Capital
- Simon Moffatt, Founder and Research Analyst at The Cyber Hut
- Stan Golubchik, Co-Founder and CEO at ContraForce
- Steve Zalewski, startup advisor and angel investor, previously CISO at Levi Strauss & Co.

- Ted Julian, Co-Founder and CEO at a stealth-mode cybersecurity startup, previously Co-Founder of @stake, Co-Founder of Arbor Networks, and Co-Founder of Resilient
- Travis McPeak, Co-Founder and CEO at Resourcely
- Uri May, Co-Founder and CEO at Hunters
- William Lin, Co-Founder and CEO of AKA Identity, Co-Creator and Board Chairman of Security Tinkerers, previously Founding Partner and Managing Director at Forgepoint Capital
- Yochai Greenberg, Co-Founder and CTO at Nano Cyber Solutions

Without the kindness of hundreds of people from the security community, I doubt that "Cyber for Builders" would make it into your hands. In moments like this, I am reminded that it is not the next-generation technologies but the people in the security space, and their passion, kindness, and willingness to help that will enable us to defend our data, infrastructure, and the world order against adversaries.

About the Author

Ross Haleliuk began his journey as a co-founder of a B2B edtech before building a decade-long career as a product leader across multiple industries, ending up in cybersecurity. His areas of expertise include go-to-market and product strategy, strategic positioning, product-market fit expansion, growth, operations, and fundraising.

Ross is currently a Head of Product at LimaCharlie. LimaCharlie's SecOps Cloud Platform provides customers with comprehensive enterprise protection that brings together critical cybersecurity capabilities and eliminates integration challenges and security gaps for more effective protection against today's threats.

Outside of work, Ross is a startup advisor, speaker, and angel investor. He often writes about cybersecurity industry trends, building security startups, investment, and growth on the world's leading media platforms such as TechCrunch, Forbes, and VentureBeat, and in his blog Venture in Security.

Ross is always happy to connect with ambitious and driven early-stage and aspiring founders passionate about building the future of cybersecurity.

Printed in Great Britain
by Amazon

35740676R00136